GW00357682

Totally Ted!

Also by Ted Sherrell:

Kingdom of Cain
The Lonely and the Lost
Milltown
A Bitter Wind from off the Moor
Nor the Years Condemn
Point of Order, Mr Chairman
And the Days Grow Short
Fire and the Phoenix
The Cutting of Mary Park. . . and Other Devonshire Tales
Looking Towards the Tamar – More Tales of Devonshire Life
Back to the Tamar – Country Tales from Early Post-War Days
From the Banks of the Tamar – Stories of Country Characters
                                   from the 1950s

Totally Ted!

Witty Reflections on Modern Life from a Grumpy Old Westcountry Man

TED SHERRELL

Illustrations by
Becky Sheppard

UNITED WRITERS
Cornwall

UNITED WRITERS PUBLICATIONS LTD
Ailsa, Castle Gate, Penzance, Cornwall.
www.unitedwriters.co.uk

British Library Cataloguing in Publication Data:
A catalogue record for this book is
available from the British Library.

ISBN 9781852001834

Printed and bound in Great Britain by
United Writers Publications Ltd.,
Cornwall.

To my beloved Ann,
who has put up with this 'Grumpy Old Man'
for almost half a century,
and to my lovely family,
for all their patience,
tolerance and love.

The *Totally Ted!* columns originally appeared
fortnightly in the Tavistock, Okehampton, East
Cornwall and Princetown Times newspapers.

Contents

1

Jargon & Prevarication

*I*N the commercial, business and banking worlds, there are certain phrases which appear to pop up like daisies an a lawn – young executives are not encouraged to do anything as banal as to pursue their careers with diligence and imagination, rather it is suggested they indulge in 'blue sky thinking' or 'think outside the box'. This is the same thing, of course, but it tends to sound a little more sophisticated and 21st century.

The companies also ensure a 'spade' is never called as such; if profits are down, expenditure up and decline threatens, there will be little mention of redundancies, closing of offices or factories – no, official statements will speak of 'rationalisation', the organisation 'changing tack' or 'regrouping'. Only in the fine print will the pain be spelt out – the loss of jobs, the physical shrinking of the company.

Most other spheres of life which dominate our national scene such as health, education, the arts and leisure, sport, the law, also indulge in this sleight of hand. Those in control must always appear to be just that and assuredly never responsible or to blame in any way for things going awry. There are occasions, especially in the emergency, health and caring services, when things really do go wrong – sometimes in calamitous fashion, and for which the powers that be cannot eschew responsibility. At such times jargon is jettisoned, usually replaced by the simple statement 'lessons will be learnt'. The problem though, is that so very often they are not!

National and local government, of course, have never been backward in the use of clever jargon – mainly aimed at the avoidance of taking action or spending money. Governments have at their disposal many ways in which they can appear to be diligent but are, in reality, doing little – Green Papers, select committees, private members' bills, courts of enquiry and, supreme among them all, the setting up of Royal Commissions. The former Prime Minister, the wily Harold Wilson, said back in the 1960s that 'Royal Commissions took minutes and lasted years', an expanse of time which often suited him and, no doubt, many other governments.

At district level policies are adopted but so is the 'fools rush in' syndrome. Thus long-term consultation takes place, corporate and strategic plans for years to come are formulated and put together. The problem is that so often by the time such plans are in place the world has moved on – and the process starts all over again.

At town and parish level, affairs are not as complicated – but again it is not always easy to make decisions, especially where it might upset a goodly proportion of the electorate and siphon money from the council tax payers' pockets. If time needs buying though there are a couple of ways in which it can be done by means both practical and

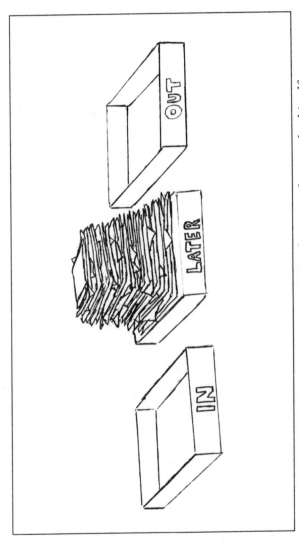

With enough prevarication sometimes the matter has resolved itself...

democratic – such as the setting up of a 'working party'. It's not hard to decide on this for if an issue brings consternation – worse, total indecision – to a committee, then the only way forward is to propose that a small group of members meet in the future, discuss the matter at leisure, and report at a later date.

Sometimes the date is so much later that the matter has resolved itself anyway – an excellent solution. The weakness with it, though, is that there are times when the problem doesn't evaporate – thus there comes a 'crunch' time when it has to be confronted.

In recent years however, an inspirational word has entered the local government vocabulary – and one which the councillor who wants a quiet life (and wishes to avoid decision at all costs) treasures; three syllables of salvation – 'monitor'. A problem is brought to the council – a solution is required and public money, probably, needs to be spent; a glance around the chamber sees councillors' eyes glazing over, their heads shaking, blank expressions upon their faces; what to do? A sharp member will move that the situation be 'monitored'. Instantly a shoal of arms will be thrust into the air in support. An admirable solution, for it means that no decision is required for the time being – if ever – no councillors will have to meet to discuss it, no money is being spent; yet the council is not ignoring the issue. On the contrary, it is constantly under review – it is being 'monitored'.

Mind you, not all issues can be 'monitored', there are some which need urgent attention – the level of councillors' allowances, for example.

2

Prejudice

SOME years ago I had the privilege of working with a most courteous, civilised gentleman, a veteran of the Second World War. He was a man of progressive and liberal views, who looked upon the world around him with, generally, approving eyes.

When, though, a few drams of 'Scottish wine' had passed his lips he would, quite regularly, opine that the brace of things he disliked most in this world were 'racial prejudice and Germans'.

At the time I though it merely a sharp line on his part – he was ever a witty man – but looking back, I have a feeling that he meant it and could see no illogicality or inconsistency in such a statement. Perhaps he was acknowledging the fact that prejudice is a normal, natural feeling – and emotion – one shared by virtually all of us; it is probably as common as love, devotion, desire, hope, joy – also, sadly, hate and despair; and as long as one is aware of it in oneself, it can do little harm.

Personally I would have to admit to possessing

prejudice in abundance, many totally illogical, some pedantic, a number probably unfair.

There is, for example, the widespread use of the American word 'Hi' rather than the good, solid English 'Hello'; centre, so often spelt incorrectly; the ancient rank of lieutenant pronounced 'lootenant' (and by British people); likewise the spelling of so many words in our land in the transatlantic way.

This, though, I must concede, is only the beginning; why do we have to put up with footballers who argue constantly with referees, with men – usually, but not always – who are basically reasonable people but after a few 'bevvies', just want to have a fight; with comedians of both genders on television – radio as well – whose abilities are so limited they have, seemingly, to rely on foul language and crudity to entertain; with people who walk dogs but fail to clean up after them; with parents who allow their children to run riot in public, doing nothing to discipline them though they are upsetting others?

But enough of this – I could go on for eternity about my foibles, those things which annoy this rather intolerant man but which, generally, to be fair are not dreadful and rarely against the law.

If I added the prejudice harboured by members of my own extended family, peaceable, fair minded group though they are, plus the full gamut of my own – then a volume the thickness of '*War and Peace*' could well result.

Sadly, there are, though, prejudices which are less harmless; at school, there was a teacher who insisted that nobody should write with their left hand – cruel, to say the least. And there are still a surprising number of folk in this land prejudiced against gays, failing, for some reason, to recognise that such a lifestyle is not chosen, but dictated by nature.

Likewise, disabled men and women often are victims of discrimination – treated as second class citizens and denied respect. There are, mind you, groups such as gypsies, new age travellers and the like, who while undoubtedly suffering prejudice, often can invite it to a degree by their own lack of respect for the lifestyle of the great majority of people; and my old friend and colleague's dislike, and more, of Germans could assuredly be justified – likewise that against the Japanese; can anybody ignore the multitude of war memorials throughout this great land of ours?

Clearly the inhabitants of these two belligerent nations cannot now be held to blame for the sins and barbarities of their grandparents – possibly even a generation beyond this. The heinous crimes of their forbears cannot, though – and certainly should not – be forgotten.

Still, while prejudice can often be a destructive force there are times when it is, in a sense, positive; where, after all, would any self-respecting football supporter be without such feelings of disdain – albeit, generally benign – towards the followers of other clubs.

As a loyal, long suffering member of the Green Army, I have been sustained by feelings of intolerance towards those misguided souls who follow other sides; some, I have heard it said, even support Exeter City; after such a shocking revelation as this, further words, I'm afraid, elude me.

3

Journey to Hong Kong

*A*IR travel has never bothered me. The opposite, in fact. For I find it can be quite relaxing sitting in an aircraft with films to watch, tea, coffee – and the occasional alcoholic beverage – to drink, and the odd meal to consume (not usually of Michel Roux standards but generally – in my view – better than its downbeat reputation would suggest). And, of course, somebody else does the driving.

The problem though, in our crowded isle, is actually getting to airports. Then, once there, navigating the convoluted maze which, seemingly always, lies between the entry doors to the terminal and the Holy Grail of an actual seat on the plane.

This daunting challenge had to be confronted recently when Ann and I set off from our Tavistock home to visit our son and daughter-in-law in Hong Kong.

The epic journey began on a cold, wet winter morning when a thoughtful grandson Tom collected us and dropped us into Plymouth to catch the 10am coach to Heathrow from Bretonside bus station – which has all the charm of a

Korean gulag. There were few about – too few from our point of view; for a number were due in from Cornwall but it was their late arriving by coach, held up because of a fallen tree, that prevented ours getting away on time.

The delay became relevant when our driver told us that the coach we were on went, actually, to Newcastle and that we would have to change at Bristol. Still, he was hopeful we'd make that city in time for our connection. His confidence was not misplaced and we duly arrived at Bristol bus station (surprisingly small and cunningly concealed) though with little time to spare.

It was then I was struck down by 'old man's disease' – not helped by excessive intake of liquid. The 'Gents' was situated on the far horizon but the attempt had to be made. Eventually I arrived but was threatened with potential 'mugging' – a sign demanding 20 pence for its use. My instinct was to raise a brace of fingers to the demand and return whence I came; my bladder said otherwise. I did though, have to make a swift return due to a lack of a 20p.

When I got back to Ann, I found her loading our luggage aboard the Heathrow coach – thus no time for the toilet. Not to worry though, the coach, of course, had its own 'loo' (something I should have thought of). Thus my health was restored, free of charge.

The coach – for some reason displaying Gatwick as its destination – got us to terminal five in reasonable time. This terminal was new to us, it not having been built the last time we were at Heathrow, but it seemed to stretch for miles.

We were checked on by a fellow possessing all the sense of urgency of the Trumpton Fire Brigade, before at last being able to proceed to the security area. Ann sailed through, not a 'beep' in sight. However, despite depositing a mountain of possessions and clothes in a tray provided – plus loose change – I managed to activate a cacophony of sound. There was urgency all around, and suddenly I had the feeling I was surrounded by almost an armed response unit – imminent incarceration appeared to be a possibility.

A very severe, gaunt looking gent, albeit courteous, had me in and out of scanners, then subjected me to a rigorous search. Finally, but I felt with a touch of reluctance, I was permitted to proceed.

A beverage was needed desperately, so off we went to a nearby Starbucks. The order was put in but what we received bore little resemblance to it. Still, it was most pleasant, clearly quite exotic, and obviously far more expensive than that we had paid for, so not cause for complaint.

Eventually we saw the number of our departing gate and set off on an epic journey involving lifts, escalators, stairs, miles of corridors and walkways, two wrong turnings, plus a stint on a shuttle train.

Viewing, at last, our departure area was a moment of bliss; almost there – but not quite – as so many others were called to board before us. At last we sat aboard the Jumbo Jet awaiting take-off.

It had taken 12 hours – many fraught – to travel 200 miles from Tavistock. The upcoming 8,000 to Hong Kong however, would take no longer to cover, and would prove to be entirely stress free.

4

Hong Kong Holiday
Part One

*H*OW does one describe Hong Kong? Well naturally, people visiting will form conflicting views. I doubt if anybody could ever say it was not somewhere they will always remember, somewhere very different – perhaps unique.

It is, in size, much smaller than West Devon yet it is one of the great financial centres of the world and has a population of more than seven million. How, one must ask, can any area so tiny, house and indeed sustain, a population of this magnitude?

Simply, because essentially, people do not live side by side, but on top of each other in high-rise apartments and flats. There are hundreds of skyscrapers as far as the eye can see. Some are clearly the dwellings of the wealthy, others shrouded in poverty.

There are no suburbs, no urban sprawl as we know it. Beside the skyscrapers are forested hills, mountains, in some instances no more than 20 yards away. This, which is as modern and sophisticated a city as the world can produce, is surrounded or interspersed by a rough, natural terrain. It was a location that fascinated Ann and myself on our recent visit there to see our son Matthew and family.

The city itself teems; everywhere there are people – clearly ranging vastly in terms of prosperity and prospects, but all busy. Everybody, everywhere, seem to seethe in constant motion. This was exemplified memorably by a sprawling street market.

The range of goods and produce on sale was immense. The crowds are so dense and jostling they make Tavistock's Goose Fair day appear about as manic as a vicarage sale of work.

Hordes thronged around countless stalls selling fish – certainly fresh as most were alive – cooked meats, birds of all descriptions, live and dead, fruit and vegetables varying from the exotic to the universal, flowers of vibrant colour, some exceedingly large. On one stall there was even a sizeable bag of writhing frogs, the fate of which was not apparent (but long life seemed unlikely). There was bread, delicacies, take-away food of all descriptions, all with hygiene standards which would drive a British health inspector to seek counselling.

Yet, just yards away from this pulsating mass of humanity, there were temples and formal gardens where one could find peace and virtual solitude. Most places one went however, there were perpetually an awful lot of people milling around, though traffic was not as dense as might be expected in such a constricted area. Public transport being very cheap – and good – many do not bother to own a car. A goodly number, of course, can not afford to. This helps enormously, leaving the roads to be travelled by numerous red taxis, hordes of 4x4s – Land

Rovers very prominent – and a multitude of Mercedes, Jags, and Porsches with the odd Maserati thrown in.

The British influence is still overt. English and Cantonese Chinese are the languages used, while virtually all the infrastructure was built during the 150 years of British colonial rule. A prime example is the cable car built during the reign of Queen Victoria. It transports people from a teeming, ultra modern shopping mall at the bottom to 'the peak', one of the highest spots in Hong Kong.

We went up partly for the experience, but also thinking we would enjoy a modicum of solitude at the top. That plan, though, went awry, as we alighted from the car to be confronted with another ultra modern shopping complex, plus traditional oriental eating houses such as McDonald's and KFC.

And, of course, the place was awash with people – walking, viewing, shopping, dining, working. No chance of meditation here. Assuredly no such opportunity would arise during the four day celebrations of the Chinese New Year which took place during our stay. This though, was glorious fun. The start of the Year of the Horse was marked with a cacophony of noise.

Fireworks exploding, bands playing, crowds singing and cheering, loud speakers blaring.

And the colours! Everywhere was the vivid, traditional red and gold in the ubiquitous decorations, in people's costumes – women and men alike – and the glorious firework displays, plus firecrackers and, naturally, the odd wandering dragon.

Still, being a traditionalist, I did miss singing *Auld Lang Syne*.

5

Hong Kong Holiday
Part Two

*T*HERE can never be pleasure without pain – not as far as we British are concerned, at least.

We had enjoyed several excellent days savouring the splendid hospitality of our son Matthew and daughter-in-law, Avisa, cocooned by the gentle, soothing temperatures of a Hong Kong winter.

Every day it was the mid to upper sixties Fahrenheit, the sun shone and clouds were seen as often as snowploughs. Not that we just laid about relaxing – that would never do. Every day we did something different, absorbing the culture, seeing the unique layout and terrain of this fascinating place, visiting the grandchildren at school; watching them play sport and so forth. We even went for a few, quite, gentle walks – one around a reservoir which, even though it had not rained in three months, still appeared to have copious amounts of water remaining.

To a man like myself, brought up in an area with one of the highest rainfalls in Western Europe, yet which, certainly in my youth, spent a majority of summers prone to water shortage, this is one of the wonders of the world.

The most densely populated place on earth, a miniscule hinterland about it, more than seven million souls to supply everyday – yet never a shortage.

On the second day of the Chinese New Year celebrations – there are four consecutive days of public holidays – Matthew sprang his surprise.

'We're going on a hike today – the Dragon's Back Trek.'

Now one of my many faults is that so often I do not really listen to what people say; the word 'trek' should have activated alarm bells; a stroll, or even a walk, has very different connotations to a 'trek'; that's what the Boers did across hostile territory in South Africa in the 19th century; similarly did Mao Tse Tung lead his rebel Communist forces over thousands of miles of Chinese terrain in the 20th – and a Dragon's back has deep ridges, down – and up.

Still, we set off in good spirits which were not dampened when Matthew said the day's hike would be a touch harder and longer than those we had done before; a touch? The understatement of the year!

We arrived at the designated place for the day's enjoyment (by bus, remarkably cheap in Hong Kong); for several seconds I stood transfixed – there lay before us, stretching upwards, something akin to the north face of the Eiger. I considered, seriously, absconding to a nearby coffee shop, but was soon dragooned into line by three fearsome grandchildren all, seemingly, with the agility of mountain goats – and, to be fair, Ann, Matthew and Avisa are no slouches either.

I managed to slot in at the rear and fortunately there were frequent halts to our upward progress as the narrow

The word 'trek' should have activated alarm bells!

path had, seemingly, half the population of Hong Kong upon it – or, at least, the European and American section. It is said the Chinese are inscrutable – clearly they are also wise, as mainly they left this fearful trek to the mad men and women from the West.

A number of trekkers, to be fair, seemed quite comfortable with this masochism, but a majority exuded little but exhaustion and misery. There would, true, be the occasional respite of a downward inclination to the path – ever rough, rocky and treacherous – but mainly it was up, up, up until the will to live had almost disappeared.

There were refreshments – sandwiches, tea, coffee, biscuits – of that I was sure, as I had seen them packed, and it was the thought that surely at some stage they would appear which sustained a semblance of discipline in rebelling legs. Then hallelujah – a magical sign written in both Chinese and English (as all are), 'Picnic area.'

The first coffee sailed down, to be instantly followed by tea; then a couple of sandwiches – life was returning to a shattered body – albeit painfully slowly.

Then, suddenly, a surreal moment, a magical instant – assuredly an unforgettable one.

Coming towards us along the track was a group of youngish fellows; one though, stood out – or rather his shirt did.

It was green – 'The Green'; across his chest the sponsor's name was emblazoned – 'Bond Timber' – beside it, the Mayflower Crest.

It was akin to Stanley meeting Livingstone; an Argyle supporter – in this desolate place. My will to live had returned – strongly.

25

b

6

Plymouth Argyle
The Traumas

'LIFE is just a bowl of cherries – don't take it serious, it's too mysterious'. These are the first lines of a famous song penned in the 1930s – and I believe there to be much truth in them.

In fact, someone I know once said that if you take life too seriously then you might want to end it all. This, mind you, would be an extreme reaction to the harsh reality which can be this existence – especially for some folk who seem so often to be denied good fortune and, at times, decent health. Still, to an extent, I go along with his view and the words of the song.

By taking life as it comes, accepting its absurdities, inconsistencies, vagaries, inequalities, even, at times, its injustices and unfairness, and seeing the funny side (often there is one), mainly living for the moment can be a quite pleasurable experience. Having said this, I do demur from this philosophy if it is suggested absolutely nothing in life is serious; to me there is one aspect that is of major gravity and has no scope for levity – football in general and Plymouth Argyle in particular.

26

My father was a good man, only callous to me once in his life – an unthinking act on his part, not for some reason visited upon my two brothers; back in 1952 he took me to Home Park as a boy of 10 years and sowed the seeds of what, for me, have been more than 60 years of addiction to trauma, stress, worry and misery, the price paid for being a loyal trooper enlisted in the 'Green Army'. There have, true, been moments of joy, but too few, too rare; for most of my life the location of the Pilgrims in various league tables has been akin to my own in terms of position in class when I was at school. To my shame, however, I always worried more about Argyle struggling on the football pitch than I ever did about my own lack of attainment in the classroom.

I have to concede that events at Home Park have always weighed too heavily with me. 'Out damn spot', cried a distraught Lady Macbeth. It could be that many a beleaguered Pilgrim fan will entreat, 'out damn club', in moments of desperation after yet another poor display – or worse – defeat. Yet, as dedicated supporters of most clubs will say, there is nothing you can do about it – football is a 'tribal game'.

When my father took me to Home Park all those long years ago he, in effect, initiated me into the 'Argyle Tribe' and, one feels, there is only one means of escape (and I'm still a bit too young to welcome that).

There have been times when I've felt cheated in that I was not born in or near places such as Manchester or Liverpool, or, of course, London. Such cities produce teams which can so often bring joy to their followers. Trundling out to Home Park, however, is little to do with pleasure – more to do with character building and, possibly, down to a misplaced sense of loyalty.

Still, supporting the biggest club in the South West, perhaps I should give thanks that I was not born in Exeter, Torquay or Yeovil (although the last club do have the good grace to wear green shirts – the only other outfit in English league football to do so). Whatever, the die was cast long ago and there will be no reprieve now; spirits, mood, outlook, mindset from August to May are shackled to Argyle's result on a Saturday (in a really nasty week, a Tuesday also).

Few personal calamities can depress if the Pilgrims have won whilst the winning of the lottery would not be quite the same if they had lost (well, perhaps a touch of exaggeration there). Thus recent years have seen an almost constant miasma of disconsolation about my person – especially at weekends – the seemingly endless fights against relegation (not always won) having taken their toll.

At present there does seem to be, at least, a glimmer of possibility that the latter weeks of this campaign will not be as traumatic as those of recent seasons.

If, however, fresh storm clouds of failure roll back in the future, I will not, in my family, suffer alone. For to my shame I have done to my sons what my father did to me; my taking of them to Home Park at an early age placed them upon the nerve-racking roller coaster of support from which there is no alighting. Still, as I get ever older and contemplate the hereafter, I do console myself with the thought that if there is a heaven, then a lifetime of following the Pilgrims must bring reward.

For if I stand before St Peter at the 'Pearly Gates' wearing an Argyle scarf, surely that Christian man will not, after my lifetime of suffering, be so cruel as to turn me away. Still, I'll not worry too much – I've friends in both places.

7

Village Life

OF all the futile exercises that can be indulged, there are
few more pointless than looking back to one's earlier
years with nostalgia. No harm in remembering the past,
mind you – especially the mistakes made; after all, if one
does not recall, and learn, then they are destined to be
repeated. However, it is surely important not to compare
then and now in critical fashion, but rather to note the
differences for good or ill – and each era possesses both.

What we are talking here, essentially, is social history, the
constant shifting sands of human behaviour, beliefs, priorities, ways of life, character, prejudice, ambitions and desires.

I was born, bred and brought up on the Bere Peninsula
back in the 1940s and 50s. It was a tight knit, largely self
sufficient community, with many of the families having
dwelt there for generations; assuredly the transience of
people in this day and age was not to be found. Such was
true of many rural parishes but being a peninsula, Bere
was probably more insular than most. The bulk of the
needs of residents of the villages and hamlets, plus the
economically important farming and horticultural entities,

29

were met. To be found were a butcher, baker, barber, post office, grocer, pub, newsagent, fish and chip shop, chemists, taxi, blacksmith, coal merchant, church, chapels and so much more, including a main line railway station, which made up, to some extent, for the poorish roads – and there was a film show in the parish hall, weekly. Thus the satisfactory cohesiveness of the parish was down to the contributions of many.

Looking back, though, there were three locals who, possibly, were more pivotal to the welfare of the citizenry than others – those who looked after the body, the soul and the law. The first was in the hands of an able doctor who, being an ex-Army medic, assumed that anyone reasonably young seeking his help was usually malingering; so sympathy from him was rare. Mind you, he had little time for such as he was a 'one-man band' – no partners, receptionists, nurses or the like; his surgery was in his own house along with a waiting. room to which one went, without making an appointment, if needing his professional advice; on rare occasions he would have a locum, but most of the time he was on call 24/7 (in modern jargon).

Matters of faith were, to an extent, the province of the Church of England rector. However, unlike the doctor he was not alone in administering to the spiritual needs of a diverse local populace with a healthy percentage of sinners. For whilst he was the representative of the established church, the peninsula was strong non-conformist country; there were about the parish no fewer than five chapels in the care of two ministers – Methodist and Congregational.

The vicar, though, was 'a character'; often this description can bestow upon someone a better image than

30

they deserve, but in this gentleman's case it was a positive word to portray a man of personality, originality, integrity, geniality – with no small measure of eccentricity. In an age when 'men of the cloth' (and they were always men) were so often 'tee-total', this gent would often frequent the local hostelries, did the football pools on a regular basis and enjoyed dancing and watching sport. What further endeared him to his 'flock', was his power as a preacher. Those were the days when congregations relished articulate sermons voiced with passion – especially those delivered on the subject of 'hellfire and damnation'; such appealed to non-conformists particularly; thus did, on occasions, a number of them forsake chapel services to attend the Anglican church and listen to the vicar 'giving them hell!'

As to law and order, most villages had a policeman, the actual station usually being in the house where dwelt the officer and his family. The constable on the peninsula was posted there as a relatively young man during the 1930s and remained until his retirement in the early 1960s.

His was a 'light touch on the tiller' when it came to law enforcement; a zealot he was not. He seemed to be possessed of a philosophy that a 'blind eye' could often be turned towards activities which, whilst not strictly in accordance with statute, did little harm to anyone else. He would have written so rarely in his official notebook, it is doubtful he ever used more than one during his career. Yet, nearly always, was he able to keep the peace.

There is no police house – or officer – on the peninsula now, and whilst a rector remains in residence, medical cover comes from Tavistock; the realities of modern life, yes – but progress?

8

'Are You Still on the Council?'

*A*RE you still on the Council?' Six simple, straight-forward words; a perfectly fair query – yet they can send a chill down the spine. For such a question, if answered in the affirmative, will not then be followed by praise, by a ringing endorsement of the excellence, wisdom and vision of the elected representatives of the local population. No commendations are about to be handed out to them; no praise forthcoming regarding noble, hard-won processes or grassroots democracy.

The opposite; for the question will be asked by a council taxpayer in tones which vary from concern to annoyance, frustration to despair, anger to outrage. The nature of the complaint or problem can be – on a good day – just irate observation, but on a bad day a furious, didactic lecture.

It will vary from the minuscule to the mind concentrating, the absurd to the alarming. A dog fouling outside somebody's house – 'Where's the dog warden?' Heaven knows – he disappeared before Lord Lucan.

'We never see a road-sweeper where we live.' Sadly,

unless one lives in the middle of town, human road-sweepers are virtually extinct. There is, though, a rather strange looking machine, with left-hand drive, which trundles round the streets and roads, vacuuming. The problem, though, is that where cars are parked, the machine cannot go. Mind you, there was once a complaint from a gentleman that his street was swept far too often – one for the archives, that.

'Have you heard they're going to build 500 houses on the Meadows – what's the council going to do about it?' Have a collective nervous breakdown, I suspect.

'My next door neighbours are playing pop music all night.' A tricky one this; rarely a police matter, usually an environment officer from the district council will recommend that the situation be 'monitored', with a record kept of times and days when the racket is at its loudest. The miscreants will probably have moved long before any action is taken – or the complainants.

'Here, what's all this about Plymouth extending and taking in Tavistock?' or 'Is it true the council is going to turn the town hall into a Wetherspoons?' or 'I hear there's witchcraft going on up on Dartmoor – can't the council stop it?' or 'Why don't they pave over the Tavy and put a multi-storey car park on top?'

All these questions have been asked in seriousness – answers having been a touch difficult to give. A real classic was the statement from one fellow a few years ago: 'There's a dead sheep in the gents' toilet in the Square –' and there was. How it got there remains among the great mysteries of the town.

'When are you going to move the war memorial as

promised?'; 'Surely you're not going to move the war memorial are you? It's fine where it is.' Both views are often heard.

And the roads: 'There are potholes in our road so deep they've got their own wildlife'; 'There's been roadworks out our way for so long, the traffic lights are due to be listed'; 'We need speed cameras in our road; somebody went through there yesterday faster than Jensen Button.'

Then there's planning; anybody volunteering to be on a planning committee should automatically have their names entered onto the Queen's birthday honours list. Self-interest and hypocrisy so often rule: 'I'm outraged my next-door neighbour has applied for a house to be built in his garden; a gross over-development of the plot,' from a gentleman who only a few years before had applied for, and been granted, permission to construct the like in his own.

Some, a touch more shrewdly, will oppose on the grounds of road safety (extra traffic); also it could have an adverse effect on the environment, could lead to flooding, plus an unsustainable strain on vital services such as water and sewerage. Nothing, of course, regarding the 'not in my backyard' syndrome. And, possibly most prevalent, there is the illogical; like the lady recently who opined in strident terms 'We don't want another supermarket in the town,' then went on to catch the free bus to Tesco at Roborough. It is, though, the democratic process that world wars were fought for, that so many Britons died for. It is precious.

9

The Terror of Technology

*I*T is to my shame that due to a craven terror of technology I eschew the benefits – or rather, the use of – that wonder of modern science, the computer. I am, mind you, quite content to take advantage of the technical ability (wizardry, it often seems to me) of others, which makes me, frankly, a hypocrite.

Having said this, I've no ambition to change my ways. It is to me a white, all-knowing monster sat in the corner of a room glaring out at us all, perhaps preparing to take over our world. That's if it has not done so already.

It took me a great expanse of time to master the biro and that will remain the limit of my accomplishments, though a sense of guilt regarding my terror of computers will stay with me.

Mobile phones, however, are a different matter. I do possess one of those, a kind gift from one of our sons many years ago. I do not, though, ever carry it or use it. There is no real ideological reason for this, rather being a solitary sort of chap, I value that very thing – solitude. Frankly, I never want to be easily contactable. I don't want the phone buzzing with people telling me their problems or giving me bad news. Sometimes, of course, one can receive good tidings over the phone, but experience shows it is usually not the case.

We have a phone at home, naturally, and have embraced the communication revolution courageously by having had installed an answerphone. Surely beyond that, little if anything else is needed.

Still, using mobile phones to talk to each other, while at times gratuitous, has to be less of a blight than its other major use – texting. Now clearly there is nothing wrong with anybody sending through a brief, important message to somebody, avoiding the complications and time-wasting of a phone call for both sender and receiver alike.

The problem is that texting would appear rarely to be used for the sending of messages of either importance or relevance. Rather, it is used for a seemingly constant flow of inconsequential chatter – even nonsense. In a free society, people have every right to indulge in frivolity – they always have. They have done so, though, by use of the spoken word, by use of their tongues. Now, it is done by texting.

Recently my wife and I were walking through Tavistock when we saw coming towards us four teenagers, two girls and two lads. They were clearly a group, though not one was talking. However, they all had mobiles in their hands and were texting. Not a word was ever spoken by any of them. Possibly when they all went to their separate homes, they would then have conversed for the first time with one another – by text, of course.

The thought comes to mind that if a brutal, wicked sect

seized power in this land and wished to ensure the population were silenced, they would not cut out tongues, but lop off texting fingers and thumbs.

Obsessive texting is not a sin, and assuredly it is not a crime. It is, though, very sad in both the cultural and social senses. Regarding the former, English is the parlance of Shakespeare and the world language in this age of technology.

It is the tongue in which Elizabeth I roused the nation in the face of the Armada, in which Winston Churchill rallied a battered, beleaguered British people to heroic, and eventually triumphant resistance of arguably the most evil tyranny in history. The tongue which Martin Luther King used so memorably to tell the world of his dream.

Yet we have now a rapidly increasing number of young people – older folk as well – who speak with a hand and clutter a small screen with a bastardised, garrotted parody of our noble language.

The social and personal angle is even more serious. Numerous girls and boys, some no doubt now men and women, are increasingly unable or unwilling to indulge in the involvement and verbal intercourse essential to the maintenance of a caring, courteous, tolerant society.

All is not yet lost, but people really do need to talk more to one another – possibly starting with families.

Still, there are times when this modern practice could have its uses. A few weeks back, we were out having a pleasant meal in a local hostelry. A large group came in, sat nearby and seemingly made more noise than the numerous clientele in the Devonport end of Home Park. If only they had been texting each other instead.

10

Magistrates' Courts

A famed Sunday newspaper, now defunct, used to trumpet to its readers that 'all human life' lay within its pages. Whether such a statement was accurate would be a matter for debate but if this weekly publication felt able to promise such, then it is fair that magistrates' courts can possibly match such claims.

Granted 'all human life' is a massive claim as it covers the whole, monumental sprawl of human nature, emotion, behaviour and iniquity – but assuredly an eclectic mix of eccentric, villainous, hapless, unlucky, vulnerable, feckless, innocent, aggressive, brutal, amoral, even evil men and women, come before such courts daily. They certainly stood in the dock at Tavistock Magistrates' Court until it, sadly, closed at the end of 2000 due to Government 'rationalisation'.

Rarely did a week go past without somebody coming up with a gem – usually spontaneous and often without guile; like the fellow, charged with the relatively mild offence of speeding, who came to court – unusual in a sense for a misdemeanour which would cost him a modest fine and cause just three penalty points to be put on his licence – saying he was falsely accused, claiming as his defence 'I never speed when I've been drinking.'

There was a memorable tale from a gent charged with a far more serious offence – driving whilst disqualified. He had been convicted once before of a like crime and now faced prison. He did admit he'd done it but put forward what he considered to be powerful mitigation. He told the bench that he'd been sitting at home in Princetown, watching television; the phone went, he answered it and on the other end was his estranged wife.

She was, he said, screaming down the phone that she was being attacked most violently by her current partner, she feared for her life and begged the defendant to rush to her aid. He dropped the phone, ran out into the street and jumped into his son's car parked in front of his house – fortuitously the keys were still in the ignition.

'I never thought of any consequences,' said he, 'just of saving her life. What else could I do?' As mitigation went it wasn't a bad tale and, if true, there might have been some sympathy from the bench. After a few seconds, the chairman asked the question which, obviously, dominated the minds of all three members 'Where does your wife live?'

The reply was instant – 'Swindon' said he. Before nightfall this gentleman had become a guest of Her Majesty.

Then there was the trial for salmon poaching in the River Walkham of a chap who, along with his brothers, had spent years from early childhood extracting fish, illegally, from the speedy river. He pleaded not guilty – as did his siblings, invariably – but at his trial the local water bailiff, an old foe, gave unwavering evidence that the

Wrongly accused!

defendant was assuredly the miscreant, even though he claimed to be nowhere near the scene of the crime.

'How can you be sure it was the defendant?' quizzed the defence solicitor. 'You have stated yourself that the light was poor and the culprit was running away so you could only see his back. How could you possibly know it was this gentleman?'

'Well,' answered the bailiff, 'I have had dealings with this man for many years and I know he has, when running, a most distinctive gait.'

This brought a howl of protest from the back of the court; the defendant's mother had jumped to her feet, an expression of rage upon her face.

'Rubbish,' cried she; 'There's nothing distinctive about our gate; we live in a council house so our gate is the same as everybody else's.'

There are times, of course, when actions speak far louder than words. A clear example of this was the young man – powerfully built – who stood before the court convicted of violence. He was a serial offender, seemingly unable to stop picking fights – whether drunk or sober. The bench had run out of patience – he was going to be sent to prison. He had, though, an excellent solicitor – a young, keen, articulate, even passionate fellow, determined if at all possible, to keep his client out of jail. He pointed out, correctly to an extent, that the defendant's problem was a violent temper; if he could learn to control that then the courts would never see him again. Thus he pleaded this young man be spared custody and be given the chance to sort out his problems by being put on an 'anger management course'.

The bench was dubious but went some way towards acceding to the request – they imposed a three month sentence on the man but suspended it with the stipulation he attended, immediately, anger management sessions. If he kept out of trouble for 12 months then custody would not be imposed. Sadly, he didn't quite make it. The following Friday be was back in court, handcuffed to a prison officer. The very first hour of the first day of his course, he had thumped his anger management counsellor. That night he too was a guest of the Queen.

11

Joggers

JOGGERS tend, generally, to be solitary beings, although on occasions you will see a pair and now and again, even a pack will pass by. The plumage varies to the widest degree and is not remotely connected to gender. The fullest range of colour and shades imaginable can be found among them.

The season makes a difference, of course, as most in summer are quite lightly protected against the elements while in winter the depth of their insulation regarding the manifold challenges which West Devon and East Cornwall can inflict is naturally thicker.

There is here, though, a much wider range in terms of bodily protection. Some, perhaps of a hardier or at times possibly a more trendy nature, will don what to the casual observer's eye could be too little over their bodies to deter rain, or worse, hypothermia.

Others, though – a majority – will appear to be well bundled up, usually with no great worry about fashion, and sometimes with insufficient regard to safety, in that they move around dark lanes and streets with little or nothing about them to shout out their vulnerable presence to passing motorists. To be fair, a goodly number do seem able to glow sufficiently in a car's headlights to make drivers aware of their presence.

Assuredly they come in all sizes – the long, short, tall, fat, thin, puny and at times (though rarely) the very large indeed. The speed at which they move also varies enormously. There are those who give the impression of progressing at a reasonable pace, as they move with some grace with a decent flowing action, legs and arms in perfect co-ordination.

Yet in reality they can at times be travelling little faster, if at all, than a brisk walker. There are others, arms and legs thrust out at all angles, heads rolling from side to side, their faces contorted like souls in torment, who cover ground at a quite respectable rate. Some likewise, who appear to be labouring, probably are. Indeed, so many who trundle along our highways and byways appear, frankly, to be in distress, their breathing reduced to gasps, their complexion the hue of overripe plums.

The first time one sees them in such a state, it is natural to feel concern over these seeming masochists, pounding along, looking to be in need of medical attention. Yet they rarely need it. So many are to be found week in, month out, pounding the same beat in their search – for what? Well, that would seem to be a fair, pertinent question.

What do joggers seek? Is it fitness? If so, then it is no easy way to attain it, though cheaper and possessing far more independence than going to a gym. Is it about losing weight? Possibly, but it is infinitely harder on the body than going on a diet.

The one element which does not come into the equation, or so observation would suggest, is pleasure.

The good, steadfast, dedicated folk who so regularly and seemingly unflinchingly pound the pavements and the lanes just never appear to look happy. Determined, yes. Exhausted, usually. Fulfilled, possibly. But happy and contented? Never.

Mind you, jogging would appear to slot neatly into the British psyche. It is said that as a nation we take our pleasures seriously. We natives of these islands generally do not feel comfortable with an easy life, with leisure that does not demand a touch of hardship or even pain somewhere along the line.

When on holiday, many a Briton will do a score of lengths in the pool, or have a session in the gym, or go on a three mile jog, or a long brisk walk, and then declare in somewhat righteous tones, 'Well, I've earned my breakfast.' Assuredly a full English one as well, after all this early morning expending of energy. What other nation on Earth has citizens who feel they have to earn a meal, especially when on vacation?

You cannot trust the efficiency of a medicine if it doesn't taste horrible – that is a mindset of many of us. Thus it could be that joggers see benefit in their purgatorial runs because they can cause pain. Whatever, long may this hardy breed enliven our rainy streets and lanes.

12

Dupuytren's Contracture

*I*F one has to suffer from an ailment then it could be argued that there are kudos if it has an impressive name.

Some ten years ago I was diagnosed as suffering from 'Dupuytren's contracture'; now while this complaint has a grandiose title, it is about as life threatening as being hit by a marshmallow and far less painful – factors very much in its favour.

A clue to its nature lies with the fact it is known in the medical profession as 'Thatcher Finger', the late Prime Minister Margaret Thatcher having suffered from it and having had it operated upon. It is relatively harmless but somewhat irritating; simply put, the little finger of my right hand, over a period of years, slowly bent into an acute angle which meant it became difficult even to fish a handkerchief from my pocket; indeed it became a major exercise to fetch out some change.

Also – somewhat embarrassingly – as it was my right hand, many folk, when I shook hands, were aware of the turned in finger and thought I was signalling I was a member of a well known organisation of a somewhat covert nature known to some, irreverently, as the 'Shake Hand Gang'. Something needed to be done – and it was.

Given a general anaesthetic (I doubt Mrs Thatcher required such, but then she was of the gender which produced the Amazons – and she was 'The Iron Lady'), my hand was operated upon and I awoke to find it quite heavily bandaged. The surgeon's view was that while the after-effects would not incapacitate me for long (it did not as I could make hot drinks that evening, write the following day and drive after three), it was probable I would one day require a repeat of the procedure; he was right.

Thus it was a few weeks ago I was again in hospital (almost a decade on, to the day) to have surgery on the very same finger. A plus, for an impatient man, was that after being told just before Christmas an operation was necessary, my time on the waiting list was brief.

A cynical member of my family, possibly correctly, opined that as the complexity of my trivial condition registered at about the same level as the removal of a wart, the alacrity of the hospital in returning my non essential little finger to a tolerable straightness was motivated by the desire of the trust to boost their statistics in terms of completed operations – it could be that half a dozen 'Dupuytren's contractures' can be completed in the same time as it takes to replace a solitary hip.

Whatever, early on a Monday morning (having consumed 'nil by mouth' since midnight) I was sitting on a hospital bed, clothed solely, and inadequately, in a flimsy gown, having a multitude of tests to ensure there was sufficient life and resilience in my aged body to endure a general anaesthetic for the brief operation to follow. Clearly readings on pulse, blood pressure, temperature and so forth suggested there was, so very shortly afterwards I found myself about to be wheeled into an operating theatre.

I was not aware of actual entry, and certainly knew nothing regarding the leaving of it. I had, however, felt as I returned to consciousness, that the process had been virtually identical to that which I had experienced a decade before. Things though, in reality, had taken a turn for the worse. My right arm was strung up to a gantry, snaking upwards like a skinny phoenix rising from the ashes; and alarmingly my hand and lower arm were encased not in warm, pliable bandages, as they had been last time, but seemingly in sufficient plaster to do a decent job to the average ceiling.

My right arm, from fingertip to armpit, was immobilised. Granted, I was discharged that afternoon and went home – but found the following days, while, to be fair, painless, exceedingly frustrating; indeed being right handed, and shamefully impatient, it was to me almost calamitous. Obviously there was to be no driving or writing.

Basics like dressing and washing became a constant challenge; the brewing of tea and coffee – both crucial to life itself – was a daunting problem, as was the carrying of cups. Without the patient efforts of Ann, dehydration would have carried me off well before my release from the wretched plaster.

After five days I did gain freedom from what felt like a paving slab encasing my arm, and was given, by a most pleasant physiotherapist, a simple range of exercises which consisted of a minute or two of splaying the fingers and a touch of thumb wiggling.

And the demon finger itself? Still somewhat bent, I'm afraid. But then, what's a minor digit, imagine going through life without a hand or worse.

c

13

Slimming

JUST before the yuletide, whilst hastening along a rain-drenched local street, I was hailed by a lady with a hearty 'Happy Christmas'. Being someone whom I'd not seen in a while we had a convivial chat during which she told me she'd just spent a lovely couple of hours at a slimming club's annual Christmas dinner.

'It was great,' she enthused. 'The food was delicious and plenty of it – and there was certainly a lot to drink.' The merry demeanour of the lady suggested the latter part of her statement was assuredly true; in fact, not only did she exude the right spirit, clearly she had imbibed a goodly amount.

After we had both passed on our separate ways, I was assailed by the thought that there was something a touch ironic about an organisation dedicated to losing weight having a feast. Surely it's a bit like somebody getting 'plastered' at the Temperance League's annual wine tasting or someone celebrating having won a peace action group's war games competition.

The world in general is full of contradictions, many

illogical, but few areas surely can match that of slimming. In this land of ours, there would appear to be three categories of folk. When it comes to pounds and stones (few, if they are of a certain age, as am I, will concern themselves with such heathen nonsense as grams and kilos), there will be those who have little in the way of weight problems, still a numerous group – despite all the talk of obesity. Then there are those overweight, or more, who are totally unfazed by such. Finally there are a goodly number rather more portly than is desirable for sound health and well-being – very occasionally to an excessive, even dangerous degree – who are determined to do something about it. So far, so good – and very wise.

There are times though, to a casual, and admittedly, untutored observer such as myself, their methods are difficult to fathom. There is, for example, that happy, dedicated group of men and women who, even on the foulest winter night, gather together, send one or two of their number off as the 'hares' (who lay a trail, usually depositing small heaps of sawdust to guide their pursuers), then chase them for miles, often in virtual darkness and on such cruel, even dangerous terrain as Dartmoor.

Eventually the hares will stop and the chasing pack will catch up with them; this though, will usually be in a hostelry where, following the exertion and subsequent weight loss of the run, sufficient quantities of quality 'John Barleycorn' will be quaffed to restore those pounds and chip away at any fitness gained. But then, this would appear to be, often, the way of things when it comes to slimming – the battle of cold common sense and intention against desire and flaccid human nature; 'The spirit is

51

willing but the flesh is weak' – or perhaps both are a touch lacking. It is for certain that the flesh is too plentiful, which is the crux of the problem. Many folk 'book' into slimming clubs or get diet sheets from doctors' surgeries and so forth, clearly feeling – understandably – that this touch of outside guidance (discipline, perhaps) will help in their pursuance of the need for a new, smaller, set of clothes. Apparently slimming clubs and groups often use a stick and carrot approach; the former, adherence to a strict diet, the latter the 'reward', every so often, of being permitted to indulge in what, to the slimmer, is a portion of food they crave.

A friend of mine – a fellow of very considerable girth – joined such a group and initially stuck well to the austere demands of the diet. However, on the first occasion he was permitted to indulge himself in a 'treat', it consisted of a pasty big enough to feed an average family for a couple of days. Still, he did at least try.

A lady I used to work with – not, in fairness, obese but certainly of ample proportions – would often be found in her office, an array of diet sheets laid before her. Beside her, however, would be an exotic collection of cream buns, cakes, chocolates and a myriad of other delicacies. Avidly did she read the diet sheets – but never adopted any of them. The culinary delights, however, were never permitted to go stale, and being someone of a kindly disposition, she would invite colleagues to help ensure such did not happen. It was a sad day when she left.

14

Prague

*B*LESSED with four good, generous sons, Ann and I recently were taken to Prague for a few days courtesy of David, twin brother of Matthew who hosted our fascinating stay in Hong Kong back in the winter.

Whilst Ann can find her way around quite well, I could get lost in Bedford Square – so being left alone in 'Wenceslas' of that ilk would have been a disaster; fortunately 'globetrotting' Dave – to whom a mere two-hour flight to Eastern Europe is little more than a commute – came with us, organising superbly our travel, hotel and leisurely itinerary.

An early evening flight from Bristol found us in our comfortable hotel by 10pm, a hostelry ideal for visitors with a total ignorance of the language, as it did not have a name but, rather, a number – 987.

The next morning, after an excellent breakfast, we went into the sunshine to explore this imposing, beautiful and very ancient city. Its history going back well over a thousand years, evocative shades of the past abound; a vast cathedral dedicated to St Vitus (who surely gave his name to a 'twitching' ailment); numerous ornate, impeccably maintained churches, almost exclusively Catholic; plentiful medieval public buildings and dwellings plus, high up, gazing down upon the city, the castle, an immense building more palace than military fortification.

Everywhere, also, there is statuary; few folk, mainly men it has to be said, who have featured in the long history of the Czech Republic – and Czechoslovakia, Bohemia and so forth (it has had many names over the centuries and too many masters) – seem to have been denied the memorial of a statue; also religious icons, carvings, mosaics, symbols, proliferate – and not just in or on churches. Public buildings, even modest dwellings have such upon their walls, or in small recesses.

Clearly for centuries this small nation – in terms of both size and population – nurtured craftsmen in stone and wood alike, wood carvers, artists, sculptors, an abundance of skilled, dedicated and talented men in these many fields. The paradox, though, is whilst this is such a cultured city giving off an ambience of tranquillity, the history of the land of which it is, and has long been, the capital, is very different.

This small state, completely land locked, has been fought for, and marched over, by armies of many different, and usually, more powerful nations – the Holy Roman Empire long ago, Austria/Hungary, Germany and the Soviet Union in more recent times. Yet strangely, miraculously even, Prague has remained virtually unscathed; it has been fought around, but seemingly never fought in.

Old photos from the mid-19th century show streets,

boulevards and facades so very similar – at times virtually identical – to those of today. Take modern traffic away, and Prague residents living some 200 years ago in the central areas (known as the Old Town and New Town, though both look much the same), could return today and see relatively little difference. They would, though, notice some Russian and German influence; the former is to be seen mainly in parts of the city built since the Second World War, which look shoddy and somewhat Stalinist; there are also museums in the centre of Prague dedicated to the 40 plus years of oppressive Communist rule – one catching the eye is the museum of the KGB (not a venue, one feels, which will be too busy).

Deutschland also looms large – great numbers of visitors and the language widely used; also, a majority of vehicles are German made, whilst the Czech Republic's own car manufacturer Skoda is now German owned. And, of course, they are both now in the European Union and NATO – close allies; certainly, this could be seen as quite surprising when considering the Nazis' brutal rule in the lifetime of many Czech people. Mind you, it could be said that the Gestapo might have learned a nasty trick or two from the medieval Czechs; back in the 14th century, when a gifted craftsman created figures of the apostles, who still make an appearance from the town hall tower on the hour when the clock chimes – to the delight of tourists – the city council, appallingly, had his eyes put out so that he could never replicate it elsewhere. Some years later an entire council, which had upset the people in some way, was thrown from windows high up in that tower. Fortunately such practices have yet to reach West Devon.

15

Progress or Nimbyism?

*T*HAT multi-talented entertainer, Bernard Cribbins, once had a hit single – a witty, highly perceptive song – 'Hole in the Road'. Among the lyrics, two lines especially linger in the memory – 'don't dig it here, dig it elsewhere, you're digging it round when it ought to be square.'

These words encapsulate so much the attitude of so many of us towards change and progress (not, it must be said, that the former guarantees the latter). Certainly, though, the first seven words really resonate regarding the reaction to it of many folk – at times an unreasonable, perhaps even hypocritical one.

For example, there are few people in our country who do not carry, and use, a mobile phone; some seem to have more such devices on them than coins in their pockets and appear to spend a sizeable portion of their waking hours speaking into them, listening or texting.

Yet so often, if the phone company – in order to maintain or improve their service – seek to site an essential mast near to where there is major use of their product, the 'barricades' are manned (or womanned). The mast, it is claimed, will be 'unsightly' – 'a danger to health, to that of children especially' – 'not in keeping with the area' (whatever that means). Thus, often it will be suggested it is sited elsewhere – out in the countryside perhaps where few live; the weakness in this, clearly, is that if there are sparse numbers to upset, then there will be few in need of the reception it will provide.

Our need for energy – electricity especially – becomes greater by the day, yet in this direction, also, the spirit of 'give and take' appears often to be dominated by the latter. Modern society devours energy in such vast quantities the danger becomes ever more real that in the future – the imminent one – demands will no longer be satisfied; modern life as we know it could be, at best, disrupted, at worst, brought to a halt.

Governments, at last, do seem to be aware of such possible calamity and are laying down plans to boost their supplies. Yet, in most directions, opposition to such schemes is immense. The cry goes out from environmentalists that 'renewable energy' is the way forward; yet mention to a community the possibility of a wind farm being set up in their vicinity, the reaction is often akin to a collective nervous breakdown, followed rapidly with a posse of folk taking to the streets brandishing placards of protest.

Nuclear power has an increasing number of advocates – it does not contribute towards global warming nor does it desecrate the landscape; and it is efficient. Yet no matter where it is proposed a nuclear plant be built, large numbers of residents within a sizeable radius of its proposed location will say it would be far better sited elsewhere.

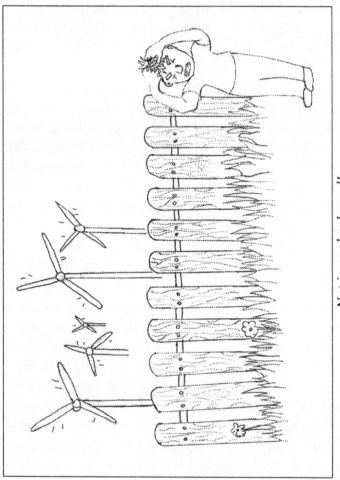

Not in my back yard!

The price of energy – high, and growing higher – concerns most of us; thus if a way can be found of obtaining fuels which will hold prices steady (possibly even reduce them), then it would bring much benefit and, one might think, be welcomed by all. Not so; for while most folk see virtue in 'fracking', too many have a reversal of opinion if it is suggested the process takes place near them. Suddenly, then, rather than bring a plus regarding the energy needs of the nation (and a possible boost to the beleaguered pockets of long suffering customers), fracking becomes only marginally less calamitous than nuclear war, allegedly creating everything from subsidence of houses to abortion in cattle, from decimation of property values to earthquakes. Rarely in any such situations will there be a mention of the 'not in my back yard' syndrome.

Yet if we in this prosperous, sophisticated, high-tech nation are not to move backwards towards the dark ages (literally), then 'nimbyism' cannot be allowed to triumph; there must be compromise. All progress surely, involves such – always has; most forward steps for the majority have been to the disadvantage of a minority. If over the centuries, such progress had not happened then we would still be living in hovels made of wattle and daub, possibly even caves, our mode of travel would be a cart pulled by oxen and all energy would be supplied by open air, wood-fuelled fires.

Mind you, there would be few 'nimbys' about – most of us would not have a back yard.

16

Magistrates

*I*F the folk who come before magistrates' courts represent virtually the full spectrum of human life, then those who judge them will also come from a manifold range of humanity – except that none will have criminal convictions as such would invalidate them.

The origins of the lay magistracy can be traced back almost 1,000 years and is unique to Britain. Men and women are from the community, appointed by the Lord Chancellor, and sit in judgement of their peers.

One of those rare areas where those appointed, in terms of gender, are roughly equal in number, this ancient office has two major qualities in the eyes of governments – it works and is cheap, with magistrates not being paid and able only to claim expenses.

These ladies and gents have always been, and remain, motivated by a strong sense of what is right, of ensuring justice is done – not necessarily the same as enforcing the law. As they come from a wide gamut of backgrounds, plus experiences – one of its major strengths – they are indeed a diverse body.

In the past, prior to the tyranny of 'political correctness' and the all too often absurdities of the human rights act, the individuality, eccentricity even, of justices were more to the fore than they are today. For example, there was a lady who was a retired schoolteacher. She seemed to take it as a personal affront if any of her former pupils came before the court.

Her blistering admonition would often be worse than the sentence the court imposed. Diversely, a lady sat for some years who was imbued with such myopic compassion that, had the Yorkshire Ripper come before her, she might well have deemed him as being misunderstood and put him on probation. Her stress levels – and those of her incredulous colleagues – were much reduced when she left the area.

Human nature and personal beliefs have inevitably conspired to ensure that magistrates often vary in their view of the seriousness of an offence. One gentleman, a man of the highest integrity with a sense of justice which could not be surpassed, being a lifelong Methodist and teetotaller tended to favour rather draconian retribution for any offence in which alcohol played a part.

Another was ever lenient in that direction. In fact, he was a charming and tolerant man in most things, treating those who stood before the court with courtesy and understanding. Such tolerance had bounds however. Burglary might not upset him too much, but being the owner of a sizeable estate, poaching did. The fellow who stood before him guilty of the illicit acquisition of a pheasant or rabbit would feel his wrath.

'Pearls', which have fallen from the lips of chairmen of

local benches over the years, abound. There was one, a farmer by profession, who was exasperated by a young firebrand guilty of a rather nasty public order offence in pursuit of obscure political posturing. He responded to the fellow's arrogant assertion that 'I do not recognise the authority of this court,' with the blunt reply 'Well your misfortune, son, is that this court recognises you.' He was sent inside for a month.

In another case, a keen young defence solicitor was rebuffed when the bench chairman, after consultation with his two colleagues and crucially their professional legal adviser, ruled against him on a point of law he had brought forward. In rather astonished tones, the young man remonstrated 'But sir, that's against all logic.'

The chairman appeared briefly surprised at such a comment, then retorted as if stating the obvious, 'What's logic got to do with it? We're talking about the law.'

Few comments though can linger longer in the memory than those of a veteran JP chairing, a few years back, a court dealing with those who had failed to pay their fines, which is ultimately an imprisonable offence.

A rather wan, dishevelled looking chap stood before the magistrates and attempted to explain why he had failed to pay anything towards the fine imposed on him months before. 'The problem is,' he said, 'I've got serious health problems, you see I'm a schizophrenic.'

The chairman, a good Devon man, gazed at him for a few seconds, a touch of sympathy upon his face, then delivered his judgement – 'Well boy, I'm sorry to hear that – but one of you has to pay.'

17

Tavistock Goose Fair

SOME, of a positive frame of mind, comfort themselves
by stating 'It's only once a year.' Those of a less
tolerant nature point out, however, (with some acerbity),
'The trouble is, it's every year.' Mind you, there are a
number of folk both within and without the town who look
forward to it, seeing it as the supreme annual event in the
local calendar.

The one certainty is that we will soon be upon it –
Tavistock Goose Fair – which seemingly since the dawn
of history has always taken place on the second
Wednesday of October.

It is an occasion which many anticipate with a measure
of enthusiasm commensurate with having a tooth out
without anaesthetic. The town is afflicted with disruption.
Even more parking restrictions abound, traffic flows are
often reversed, showmen and many traders' caravans and
vehicles clutter quiet roads and streets, and while such as
local pubs and restaurants do good business, that for many
shops is so poor they do not even bother to open.

It is arguable though that Goose Fair has at least one

great quality, a compelling reason why it should be welcomed in fact – it is possibly unique. It is unlikely that great writer John Steinbeck ever heard of it, let alone attended it, but in one of his novels he describes Cannery Row in Monterey in California as 'a poem, a stink, a grating noise, a quality of light, a tone, a habit, a nostalgia, a dream.' While this evocative prose is directed towards a very American location, it bears so much resemblance to the mayhem which takes place in our sedate old stannary town every autumn.

Assuredly it is a day of odours and decibels – 'the stink' a heady mix of pasties, fish and chips, burgers, diesel, livestock and jostling humanity while the 'grating noise' is constant, awesome and can be heard miles away. Strident music, the whine of fairground rides, blasts and bellows from livestock desperate for the peace, nutrition and space, of the lush rolling Devon pastures, the cries of the Del Boys, the 'Cheap Jacks' who at their best can provide entertainment probably superior to the goods they are selling.

And of course, the cacophony of human interaction, thousands ambling the streets, fairground and markets, talking, laughing, moaning, gazing, perhaps arguing and most crucially of all to those displaying their vast array of wares and foods, buying.

The words 'habit' and 'nostalgia' also have relevance. For such motivates many who attend the fair, they having come, sometimes, many miles, for years – perhaps decades.

A multitude will throng the streets by noon and when in late afternoon they head for home, 'the evening shift' will appear, those who for varying reasons are unable to attend during daylight hours. Again, much cash will change hands.

There will be complaints; 'Cheap Jacks' today allegedly, are rogues (whereas years ago, presumably, they were ever folk of total integrity).

The 'characters' – a much overused, ambiguous term – have all disappeared, the price of rides is exorbitant, and ever briefer.

The weather is too wet, too hot, too cold – take your pick; there are too many people about – though some will say too few; there are not enough bargains and too much junk.

The final judgement from many will be much the same as came from the lips of their parents years ago – possibly similar to that opined by many generations of their family – 'it's gone downhill; not what it used to be.'

In this, respectfully, I would disagree. It changes, yes: this is an event which reaches back centuries – it has altered to reflect an ever different world. It began in medieval times in the early years of the second millennium – we are now in the third.

Yet it retains essentially the ambience, the 'tone' of its roots. At core, it is a livestock market, an agricultural show with a strong presence of farmers and rural folk. Over the ages though, it has incorporated the flavours of a craft fair, village fête, bazaar, possibly even Petticoat Lane, and in recent times a strong presence of stalls raising funds for local charities.

In some ways, Goose Fair for many local residents can be a 'pain in the neck' – possibly also in another part of one's anatomy. Yet it remains popular, which is good for the image of Tavistock and West Devon – and is, clearly, that which is ever dear to the hearts of us British – traditional.

18

Old Age – The Plusses

FIRSTLY, an honest admission; I am an old man with the sole aim in life of becoming an even older one.

I have reached an age now when, if I hear of the demise of anybody under 80, then I shake my head sadly and mouth the words 'no age at all'. Gone fortunately are the days when anybody making 'three score years and ten' had been favoured in that they had reached what then was viewed as the far end of their allotted span. Thanks to the advancement of medical science, the life expectancy of the male of the species in this era is 80, at least, whilst the female can feel a touch aggrieved if this mortal coil is 'shuffled off' before, possibly, 85 (or, to be more exact, their loved ones can feel so).

Possibly even more importantly, the quality of life and opportunity for those of state pension age, and well beyond, is so much greater and rewarding, and, which has relevance, rewarded. Not least amongst these benefits are free prescriptions; mind you, the need for them, generally, is greater as one grows more mature, but it remains a bonus.

Then there are free bus passes; if one was to plan ahead, minutely, one could travel the length of the country and pay not a penny in fares. Not easy to achieve, mind you, as it would need multitudinous changes of buses and coach companies as one progressed through the counties, a mastery of the intricacies of timetables which could require the brain of an Einstein, the dedication of a marathon runner plus the fitness and steely resolve of a member of the SAS; but it could be done. The reality personally, however, is that my wife Ann and myself can travel in relative comfort to the heart of Plymouth, and our lunch will be paid for in what we save in fares.

On the entertainment and leisure fronts, many theatres, sporting venues and various events give reductions to pensioners (I can get into Home Park at a reduced rate, though this is very much a mixed blessing), as do, on certain days, many shops and stores.

Haircuts, too, cost less; it has to be said, mind you, that often (certainly in my case) there is far less to cut, but it is, never the less, a useful bonus. In this direction, though, I've been fortunate in a sense, for always tending to look older than my years – plus being 'follicly challenged' for decades – I've been charged a pensioner's rate since about the age of 50 (I felt no guilt over it, because I was never asked my age – the barbers just saw the worn, disintegrating features, and assumed).

Car insurance, too; is a field where benefits are to be found; usually the premiums are lower. Why this is so has to be a mystery; why, when a driver reaches an age when their sight is possibly fading, their reflexes are probably not much greater than that of a sloth, their judgement not what it was, they are, in the view of insurance companies, safer on the road than younger folk, has to be a major mystery – but long may it last.

Then – there is the old age pension; the majority of people, of course, will have earned it. Whether employed or working for oneself; decades of paying one's 'stamp' will have been involved, with no guarantee of drawing even a penny from it. If 65 can be reached, though, it is warmly reassuring to know that the Government will ensure that every four weeks to the day, a payment, automatically, will be made into one's account.

It's not massive, but not miserly either; the ambition has to be to live long enough to make a profit – to draw out more than one has put in; I've a few years yet to go in this direction but it does give an aim to life, which is no bad thing.

So despite the fact the eyes grow dimmer, the hearing duller, the hair thinner, the skin slacker, the legs heavier, the hands weaker, the mind slower, the opinions narrower, the memories vaguer, the ambitions fewer, the teeth falser, the tolerance lesser, the cynicism greater, there's nothing much wrong with growing old. It can be avoided, of course, but – not an option to be recommended.

19

Modern Fathers

*T*O men of my age, they are to be admired and respected; at times I feel they are even to be wondered at. Are they, though, to be envied? In the view of this dinosaur-like scribe, assuredly not. If there is one aspect of life which makes me both pleased and relieved to have reached reasonably advanced years it is that I, and probably most of the men of my generation, experienced, and enjoyed, the fulfilment, pride and pleasure of fatherhood – all pluses – without the, to me, minuses of actually having to look after children; especially when babies.

The fate of the 'modern father', though, is so very different. They get involved right from, indeed, at the time of birth; what to me seems worse – they want to be. Back in the 'days of yore' when my sons were born, the expectant father's most vital contribution regarding the impending birth was to get his pregnant spouse – for that, then, was usually the relationship – to hospital or the maternity home, or possibly to call the midwife. That done, he was not expected to hang around, unless he wished to, and most certainly he was not wanted at the actual birth; that was most strongly discouraged.

Most fellows went back to work, or home, or did some gardening. I know one chap who took himself off to Home Park, it being a Saturday afternoon, then went to the maternity home to find out he was the father of twin girls; whilst he'd seen Argyle lose, the day had still ended with a good 'result'.

When the expectant male parent became a real one, he would attend his wife and baby son/daughter, with both alacrity and love, hold the tiny offspring momentarily (something which filled me with terror, my ineptitude regarding holding onto a football in goal-keeping days being at the forefront of my mind). Then, when the nurse or midwife mouthed the magical words 'mother and baby need rest', he would kiss both and make for the nearest hostelry, probably with a few male friends, to 'wet the baby's head'.

Children then were largely cared for and, in their early years at least, raised by their mothers; ours certainly were – and brought up by the best. She fed them (though, in my defence, during the early months it was not a task she could delegate), did the cooking – and for us all – took care of the washing, of which there was a mountain, and accomplished it using a washing machine which now might well have a starring role in an edition of the Antiques Roadshow.

A large part of the laundry were nappies (no disposables in those times), all of them changed by their mum. Our youngest being twins – and if one cried at night, inevitably he awakened the other – I did assist as 'labourer' in the small hours, but with no enthusiasm and even less aptitude. At times, if I arrived home earlier than I meant to, I'd be drafted in to read the boys a bedtime story; so bad was I at this simple task, it quickly got that the lads would feign sleep rather than have to suffer my stilted, monotonous reading. Probably I was less involved than some fathers back then, but I fancy I was little different from the majority.

How different are my sons and their generation. Three of them have seven children between them and they have all been involved in the raising of them. All have been present at the birth of our much-loved grandchildren; can, and do, change nappies in seconds, are excellent in the kitchen – preparing good food to fill the plates of adult and child alike – are adept at washing and ironing and, impressively, seem usually to be on the same 'wavelength' as their offspring, in tune and sympathy with the workings of a child's mind.

They make time too, to play with them, to entertain them; often this is described as spending 'quality time' with their kids – as opposed, one assumes, to mediocre time (perhaps changing nappies comes into this category). It can also be known, apparently, as 'bonding', an exercise in strengthening the ties between father and son or daughter. Nothing wrong with this, of course, and modern fathers are to be applauded for being so deeply involved in raising their children.

Yet, on the whole, I don't think my generation of men did too bad a job as parents; whatever, deserved or not, my wonderful sons were very kind to me on Father's Day.

20

Cyber & an Idiot

*I*N matters technical, I have the gumption, aptitude and flair of an amoeba. Our 5-year-old granddaughter showed me, with patience beyond her years (but with no lasting success), how to operate the DVD player, whilst another young grandchild had to stand over me shooting instructions, when I was struggling, pathetically, trying to make a call on a mobile phone. As for computers, word processors and the like – well, they are beyond my comprehension; e-mail likewise. My excuse – so weak it can barely stand – is that my advanced years render me incapable of learning modern ways; the 'old dog' bemused by 'new tricks' syndrome. The problem here, though, is that there are numerous folk of like age to me – older, in fact – who can command and manipulate the most sophisticated IT with ease, authority and aplomb. For them my admiration knows no bounds; I do not envy them, however, nor do I intend even to attempt to master such arcane arts; my stress levels are ever high due to the constant psychological warfare waged by a capricious organisation named Plymouth Argyle – anything further would lead to visits by concerned folk wearing white coats.

My sole mastering – very modest – of a technical monster took place in my youth, over half a century ago. I refer to the driving of motor cars, powered, as Winston Churchill remarked (unsympathetically), by the 'infernal' combustion engine. Even in this, though, was I inept, having to take my driving test three times; so many hours did I spend meandering uncertainly – possibly even dangerously – around the streets of Launceston, I got to know the town as well as most residents. The fact, however, that I was deemed, eventually, capable of being in charge of a motor vehicle did not, and does not, mean I have any knowledge of its power source – clearly also a mystery to the great Sir Winston (though be had an excuse as he did not drive); I know how to check petrol, oil and water levels, plus tyre pressures and windscreen washers – all crucial to both the wellbeing of the car, the safety of the passengers and health of the owner's finances (especially the oil level). The bulk of the array of gadgets, hoses, cables, boxes beneath the bonnet, though, are a mystery – it's like gazing upon the surface of the moon. In theory, mind you, this should not, in modern cars, matter too much when checking if systems are working; for if there is some problem, defect or malfunction, the driver will be informed whilst sitting in the vehicle. There will be lights on the dashboard flashing merrily, a multitude of 'beeps' will assault the ears; indeed, the senses will be assailed by seemingly more illumination and sound than engulf the average town at Christmas. Whilst this seems sensible and helpful, to the dense and easily terrified such as myself, there is a major problem –

d

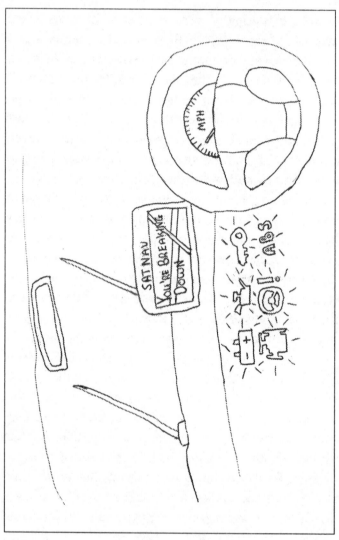

It's all a mystery when the warning lights flash!

bewildering excess. Now, if a light came on warning the engine is about to blow up, or the water is hot enough to boil an egg, or if a miniature siren wailed to warn a wheel was about to fall off, the system could not be faulted; and, no doubt, such would take place.

The trouble, though, is that the lights and sounds are not restricted to this; bulbs flash if the water is too cold, too hot, the seat belts are unfastened, a window is slightly open, the side lights are on, the handbrake likewise, power steering is working or otherwise; there is a rear fog light indicator (whatever that is), an anti-lock brake system indicator (again, a mystery), something regarding air bags, an immobiliser system indicator (the mystery continues); that the ignition key has been inserted – or withdrawn; many of these, and more, are accompanied by sounds, a cacophony akin to an Italian traffic jam. Such a barrage of noise and magnitude of illumination could easily induce irritation and indifference in the able and knowledgeable; to the mechanically illiterate such as myself, it instils, initially, terror, often to be followed by a surge of the traditional British spirit – 'Carry on Regardless'.

The problem is, of course, that while most times the tsunami of light and sound heralds no problem or danger, there could be amongst it all a small beam or 'beep' warning that an aspect of mechanics or passenger safety needs urgent attention, and it might, unfortunately, shine less brightly – or be softer in tone – than that which informs there are clouds in the sky or some like trivia.

There seems to he nothing, though, which shows how much such lights and alarms are draining the battery. All one can do is turn on the ignition – and hope for the best.

21

Christmas

*T*HERE is an old adage which suggests 'It is better to travel hopefully than to arrive.'

This is not without substance, for when going into the unknown – on holiday, say, or attending an event which has been anticipated with enthusiasm – most of us will, at times, have felt pangs of disappointment, occasionally in a major way, when reality has fallen far short of expectations. There is a journey, though, which we travel annually, where the familiar destination is far more pleasurable than the long, fraught, stressful, frustrating, at times frenetic trip which leads to it; that bleak expedition is nearing its much craved end at last – Christmas is almost here.

There is no set date when the trek commences, but early September is usually when the wearying, sometimes depressing, business creaks into motion; that is when children return to school, summer moves relentlessly towards the 'season of mists and mellow fruitfulness' and shops, seemingly overnight, became awash with mountains of goods aimed at the Yuletide. Supermarket aisles are swamped with boxes and tins of chocolates and sweets, crates of liquors, plum puddings, rich iced cakes, mince pies (all most civilised), crackers, toys, games – indeed, a vast range of products all directed at, essentially, the celebration of just one day three months hence.

Shops and stores, likewise, have stocks so vast that the 'sweat shops' of India and China will have been on overtime for months to have fulfilled their orders; and to be found in some of the larger ones, a posse of red garbed, white bearded fellows sitting in their grottos encouraging children to empty their parents' abused wallets.

Emporiums of all sizes will generally be festooned with decorations, while it is not unusual to enter a shop on a warm September day and be greeted with the soporific tones of 'White Christmas' from the lips of Bing Crosby. Ingress and egress of such will often be impaired by stacks of merchandise the purchasing of which, purveyors will claim, is crucial to the enjoyment of the festive season. So it begins – three months of nerve jangling mayhem. Yuletide now is not an event, rather an industry; if it did not exist already, it would have to be invented – the Chancellor of the Exchequer would insist on it.

'What shall we get little Jack or Jill?' will be the cry; there will be an even louder wail when it is discovered that the sophisticated computer desired costs more than a decent second hand car. And what to buy for a multitude of other family members, friends and so forth? Something that they might like, yes –which costs as little as possible. In this direction it is crucial to keep a list of gifts received the previous year; if you got nothing, then reciprocation will be the policy, surely, while someone whose gift was unwanted, unsuitable or just plain daft will not be high on the list of priorities when purchasing.

Obviously, though, they must not receive back that which they gave the previous year; thus the importance of the list – such a present needs to be recycled to a distant relative far away. The choosing, buying and distribution of gifts is only part of the stress which can build daily; there are cards to be bought, written, distributed – as many by hand as possible, postage costing more than the contents; there are decorations to put up, family gatherings to organise and external events like work, office, club parties, lunches and assorted 'booze ups' to attend.

Such can produce dyspepsia, boredom, 'punch ups', hangovers, and possibly even a dreaded invitation to blow into a breathalyser. And with the church trying to get in on things, there are those chaotic, anarchic brawls entitled Nativity plays. As youngish parents we confronted these terrors years ago, buoyed by the belief we would be exempt when reaching more mature years; we forgot about grandchildren – once again finding ourselves witnessing the wielding of shepherds' crooks as weapons of war. Hilarious – as long as you are not in range.

Finally, though, I have to make an admission; on a 'Richter scale' of hypocrisy, this article warrants the full ten. The fact is, I feel no real stress at all – because I do so little towards Christmas. My wife Ann does the planning, buys most of the food and presents (and wraps them), writes most of the cards, does the cooking – and never, unlike her husband, tries to avoid Nativities. Thanks to her, I love the Yuletide; as the saying goes 'bring it on'. Merry Christmas everybody!

22

A Cynic? – Guilty!

*T*HERE are numerous groups of people in this world with a different outlook to mine for whom I have much admiration. Well to the fore of such are those not only with a deep rooted sense of what is right (with which I have complete empathy) but also with an idealistic, unwavering belief that things can, and will, improve. Even more remarkable, in my admiring eyes, is that they eschew, unreservedly, cynicism, convinced that men and women alike are essentially noble beings and that, ultimately, mankind will create a universe of equity, justice, tolerance and compassion. No matter what evidence to the contrary manifests itself – sadly, copious amounts daily – their belief in such seems never to be shaken.

Sadly, I am, and have always been, the opposite; since boyhood, my philosophy of life has been that one hopes, naturally, for the best but expects the worst (mind you, 60 years of following Plymouth Argyle have stoked this).

While such negativity has never bothered me, I do think that it might be pleasurable, just occasionally, to feel a surge of positivity through my veins; say, on a dull morning, to anticipate the sun shining rather than expecting a gale to blow. Thinking back, though, my mother could be even more downbeat than myself, for if early morning in summer she gazed out of the window and saw blue, bright skies, she would opine – 'Sun before seven, rain before eleven'; unfortunately, being a knowledgeable countrywoman, usually she was correct. Still, one can only respect the noble, generous mindset of idealists whose belief in the inherent decency and goodness of folk is ever to the fore as is their positivity.

Cynical pragmatist that I am, probably far too often I expect the worst of people – in many instances, unfairly, even shamefully. Recently, at home, I was watching that excellent Hollywood blockbuster 'Spartacus'; at the end there is the famed scene where numbers of prisoners are lined up and it is demanded that the man himself steps forward; he does (well, Kirk Douglas, does), but no sooner has that happened, than scores of others do likewise, crying, 'I'm Spartacus'– which is where disbelief sweeps over me like a tsunami. For would not the reality be the opposite? The Romans were not noted for their leniency – chances of transgressors being sent to an open prison for a few leisurely months would have been remote; the true situation is that retribution for whoever was the leader of the slaves' rebellion would have been brutal. So is it not a more likely scenario that multitudinous fingers would have pointed at the leader, their owners crying: 'He's Spartacus' or, at best, silence would have reigned with the captured keeping their heads down, hoping for the best?

Then there are financial rewards. There was recently a

song the lyrics of which stated: 'It's not about the money, money, money'; that, though, too often, is exactly what it is about. Denials of pursuit of cash fall, regularly, from the lips of Premier League footballers; they kiss the badge of their new club, pledging undying loyalty; reality suggests that when their contract expires (often before), they and their agents will be scanning the horizon to espy an even better pay day. All too often it is only about the 'money, money, money'; and so many other situations, even when finance is not directly involved, are drenched in cynical self interest.

Here the NIMBY brigade are well to the fore. When folk object to a house (or houses) being built, they almost invariably, will articulate a host of legal and environmental reasons for their stance. Yet is not their opposition often fuelled by the selfish belief that what is proposed will in some way (often only marginally) be to their disadvantage; if what was to be built was sited a mile or so away from where they live, most would not 'give a damn'. To be fair, however, it has to be conceded that there are those who fight causes even though they have no personal interest; rather they care, sincerely, for the world and the people on it – to them quality of life, not money, is paramount.

Constantly, also, there is heroism from men and women who face imprisonment, torture, even death in defence of principle and the oppressed. Many such folk might well have cried 'I'm Spartacus'; assuredly it must be concluded that people of this calibre contribute far more to society than cynics like me. They are to be admired – and envied.

23

Cooking – A Paradox

*U*LTIMATELY it is a paradox, is it not? So many of us in this great nation spend hours each week sitting before television sets watching programmes about food, restaurants and cooking. Those highly skilled in the art are household names – the faces of Gordon Ramsey, Jamie Oliver, Gary Rhodes and the like are probably as well known as that of David Cameron (reality suggests, in this sad and dangerous age of cynical indifference to things political, they could be even more familiar), whilst those of the female gender such as Mary Berry and Delia Smith are possibly not vastly short of the Queen herself in terms of instant recognition.

Their concoctions and creations before the cameras are viewed by millions. Having the very 'sweetest of teeth' (and, in consequence, not many of them), to me some of their desserts, gateaux and the like have even greater beauty than a Plymouth Argyle victory (well, perhaps a slight exaggeration there); likewise, to many, the intricate imaginative savoury dishes are a delight to the eye.

There are also, of course, a multitude of contests of non-professionals – innovative, desirable dishes devised and created by women and men to whom cooking often appears more a religion than a hobby. 'Masterchef' is foremost among these – an enjoyable, entertaining programme which to anyone wishing to increase their knowledge, not just of cooking, but of the spices, herbs, often obscure vegetables and such like available in the world, is instructive, possibly even invaluable.

There is also, of course, *The Great British Bake Off*, which, to those of us who feel that good food should be lathered with sugar and cream, is essential, even mesmeric viewing; in fact, I'm tempted to watch this wearing a bib to catch the drool.

Clearly there can be no harm in millions of folk gazing at the 'box' watching those of greater dedication, ability, ambition and fame displaying the culinary art, giving advice and tips regarding the creation of good, flavoursome food, whilst being entertained in the process. Indeed, market researchers and pollsters whose function it is to apprise us of the way we, as a race, live and order our lives, say that British television devotes more time to cooking and general culinary matters which have, relative to population, greater viewing figures than any other nation in the world.

Also, as any bookshop owner or manager will say, cookery, recipe and allied publications are amongst, consistently, their best sellers (likewise, books on dieting – but that's another story). So where lies the paradox? Simply in the fact that the same researchers suggest that we British cook less than any other country in the western world – possibly the entire one.

The most vital, and used, appliance in numerous kitchens is the microwave, the cooker standing forsaken in the far corner – if there be one at all. The inevitable consequence of this is that, again per head of population, we devour more takeaway food than anybody else. Much of this is Asian and Oriental – curries, kebabs, Chinese dishes are hugely popular; many, though, prefer European cuisine, spaghetti, pasta and pizzas well to the fore, whilst the New World is also prominent, chilli and tortillas from Mexico, the ubiquitous burger and hot dog from north of the Rio Grande. Mind you, the Union flag still has a flutter left in it, as those traditional takeaways, fish and chips and pasties retain a buoyant market.

There is, of course, nothing wrong with consumption of dishes conceived beyond our shores; the contrary, in fact – there are superb foreign creations, many of which are to my own taste. Indeed, I must admit to being a chilli addict, whilst curries and pasta meals are always welcome.

Rarely in our house, though, are there takeaways, as I am blessed with a wife, Ann, who can create everything from chilli to goulash, curries to lasagne – and good British fare like cottage pie and roasts – all with equal expertise, all a joy to eat; no takeaway on earth will equal them.

I do, however, at this point, have to admit to being a hypocrite, being as much use in a kitchen as a cardboard saucepan. Were I not pampered by Ann, I have no doubt my dustbin would be groaning with grease saturated foil trays and paper; I would also be far poorer – and concerned over my cholesterol levels.

24

The Devonshire Method of Measurement

IT is said that the majority of we Britons of three score years and over, if required to state it in metric units, have no real idea as to how much we weigh or what is our height.

Mind you, there's no great problem when using imperial measurements – good old stones and pounds, feet and inches – but when the dastardly European system comes into play (and officially virtually everything is supposed to be expressed in such terms), bemusement and aggravation dominate. To a certain extent this applies also to those of a later generation, folk in their forties and fifties who would have learnt, officially and anecdotally, modicums of both systems.

A prime venue to witness such are builders' merchants' depots and DIY stores where people can be heard asking for, say, lengths of timber, 'two metres long and three inches wide' or 'five litres of white emulsion and a quart of turpentine.'

For some reason television programmes and national

newspapers will refer to long journeys in terms of kilometres while, officially, we still measure such in miles. After all, how often do you see a directional sign giving distances in metric terms? On the other hand, these media folk, when they finish their working stint, will probably make for the nearest pub where they will have no truck with litres and order a round or two of pints.

A further angle on measurement or distance is the fact that the performance of a car is ever advertised in terms of 'miles per gallon', never 'kilometres per litre'. Birth, too, has to be included in the nation's schizophrenia when it comes to terms of size; for babies never enter this world weighing kilos and grammes; no, folk will be told of the joyful event using traditional avoirdupois pounds and ounces. Clearly, in so many fields, confusion reigns, bringing extra and unnecessary stress to copious numbers of the population of all ages, whether they be working out weights of ingredients to bake a cake, amounts of sand, cement, blocks and so forth to build a house, volume of wool needed to knit a jumper or quantities of fertiliser to feed the lawn.

Numerous other aspects of life, basically straight-forward, require this tedious, wearying deciphering in terms of measurement.

Arguably, there is, however, a solution to this, a means by which people can be freed from the tyranny of statistical orthodoxy; the Devonshire system of gauging such matters can be mobilised.

For here in the county of Drake we have long embraced a very different, but most effective scale; granted, it is not used as widely as it was in my youth, but among rural and farming communities it is still often invoked when assessing matters and ordering requirements essential to the maintenance of civilized life.

It is a system which requires no usage – no knowledge, in fact – of official units in either imperial or metric; thus, it's both democratic and pragmatic; its purpose is to convey quantity, size, distance, in a general, easily remembered fashion without recourse to the tedious gathering and calculation of accurate measurement.

It has slight variations according to whether it relates to numbers or bulk. If say, a farmer wishes to inform of the number of sheep in a field, he will do so in a simple, succinct way which will be understood clearly by the person to whom he is talking (as long as the man or woman is versed in the system). If there are but a small number, he will use the word 'few'; a larger, but still modest gathering, will be a 'fair few'; a biggish flock, a 'brave few', while 'any amount' will be the term articulated if the meadow is teeming with beasts.

When volume, rather than numbers, needs assessing, the Devonshire method is equally adequate and effective. A haulier, for example, if confronted with soil or ballast needing removal from a building site, will not wrestle with the complexities of attempting to calculate how many tons – or tonnes – are in the heap; rather, he will know, shrewdly and rapidly, how many journeys his lorry will have to make to fulfil his task, using the local system. A small pile will be 'a bit'; a larger, but still moderate one will be a 'fair bit'; a substantial heap, a 'brave bit' whilst a mountainous one will carry the same description as that of the multitude of sheep, 'any amount' – and each assessed quantity will translate, in his fertile mind, to the number of trips his lorry will need to make. A simple method? Assuredly. An undemanding one? Without doubt. Will it ever be adopted? No. The simple, even if masterly, is never trusted. It undermines the 'experts' and the settled order of things.

25

Devonshire Dialect

*B*EING a man whose family, on both sides, have had roots embedded deep into the soil of Drake's county for at least the past couple of centuries, it is, to me, cause for concern and great dismay that the rich, distinctive Devonshire accent would seem to merit inclusion on the list of endangered regional brogues and dialects; in the media it would appear to be virtually extinct.

Flick on the television, switch on the radio and, over a period of just a few hours, numerous British accents will be heard – the somewhat nasal 'whine' of the 'Scouser', the so distinctive talk of the 'Geordies', Scottish, Welsh, Irish, both north and south of the border (very different intonations), the flat vowels of the Midlands, the sharp, rapid, flamboyant chatter of the 'Cockney', the terse, almost argumentative tones of those native to Yorkshire and Lancashire, plus many others.

The Westcountry, though – that's a different tale. Just occasionally a Bristolian burr can be detected over the airwaves – though many would argue, surely correctly, that this old city is located far closer to the Midlands than the South West Peninsula; in the media, sadly, a Devon accent and the use of local dialect words can be heard about as often as a cuckoo in January. Granted, it has to be conceded that it is a minority in our county who roll their 'Rs', have healthy contempt for the use of the letter 'H' at the beginning of a word and who employ a wide range of abbreviations and derivations unique to Devon. They are, though, still to be found; travel the numerous lanes of the rural areas well away from the cities and larger towns, and the accent is still alive and reasonably well, though probably not flourishing. Likewise to be found are an array of dialect words, some pragmatically creative, others which aid both articulation and brevity.

Devon farmers do not keep 'ewes', they stock 'yaws'; if they have a leaning towards equestrianism, they will mount an ' 'oss', a large animal possessing 'chacks' rather than cheeks, which wrinkles up its 'naws' and, if hearing a noise, pricks up its 'yers'. The word 'yer', though, can be employed as an adverb as well as a noun – for example, when attempting to gain someone's attention, 'Yer boy' or 'maid', being a polite, succinct way.

Many a local farmer, if born in the county, will not use harrows to work his hilly terrain – 'arves' will be employed. If narrow strips of soil between parallel lines of crops need weeding, a 'scuffle' will do the job. If any plants need replacing, a small hand tool, officially termed a 'mattock' but known locally as a 'vizgee', will be operated, whilst more heavy digging by hand will be accomplished using a 'sladaxe'. And just trying to locate places on a farm can lead to confusion; a milking bovine will not be found in a cowshed, but in a 'shippen' –

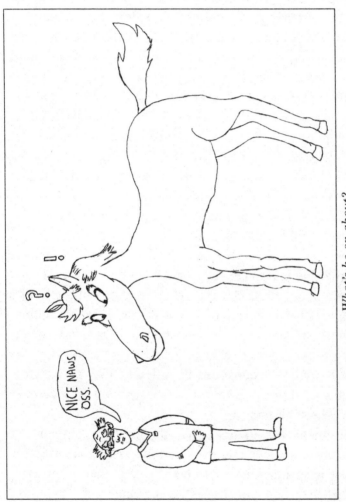

What's he on about?

assuredly she will not be housed in a 'mooey', despite the name, as this is an area close to a farmyard where are stored bales of straw and hay. Mind you, dialect words are not to be found solely amongst the farming community.

A laundry container is a 'flasket', whilst a certain sized barrel of beer in a pub, officially a hogshead, becomes corrupted to 'uggset'. A very young child is a 'cheel' or a 'little tacker' and if they grow up to be wise and intelligent, then they become 'long headed'. Other descriptions of folk, though, can be less complimentary; a person (usually a man) of irresolute character is a bit 'cakey', whilst someone with an exaggerated self regard will be condemned as being a 'blower'.

If folk do foolish things they can be classed as being 'maze' – if totally daft ones, then they are 'maze as a sheep', which can often be a slander of harmless 'yaws'; if someone is a touch eccentric, he or she is a 'case' – if considerably so, 'a brave case'. These are but a few of a comprehensive lexicon of Devon words, some corruptions of precise versions of standard English terms, others imaginative, evocative local creations which aid brevity and are fully understood. It is a pity they're no more widely used, for they by-pass verbosity, cutting succinctly to the heart of things.

It could be, though, that the modern passion for 'texting' could come to the aid of our Devon dialect; after all, it is so much easier to text, 'cakey' than to describe someone as being of 'irresolute character'.

26

'I'll Never Forget
What's 'is Name?'

*B*ACK in the 1960s, when I was a regular cinema goer, there was a British film which has lingered in my memory. It wasn't very good – in fact, to be honest, I cannot recall what it was about; what has stayed with me, though, is the title – 'I'll Never Forget What's 'is Name'.

At the time it struck me as being a clever, perceptive comment on people, life – indeed, human nature. Now, five decades on, pragmatic reality – perhaps, most accurately, cynicism – having coloured my outlook, I feel that as an observation and reflection on such, the half dozen words which were the film's title are beyond cleverness, they are profound. For, in masterly fashion, they display the brutal but eternally unavoidable, transience of life.

Mind you, it is possibly worse now, this modern age moving apace with ideas, technical advancement and innovation in abundance, also there is the flitting across the national consciousness of so called 'celebrities' – men and women who gain short term fame, in some cases notoriety, thanks to the sensationalism and superficiality of so many national newspaper reports, but who fade towards obscurity before those same dailies perform their secondary function – insulation for fish and chips.

To be fair, though, it has ever been thus to a degree, those who were mighty, at times almost legendary, names to one generation, fading to obscurity – even anonymity – in relatively short time; there are, for instance, those among us who now, sadly, think that Winston Churchill is the name of a dog which sells insurance. Likewise, some believe Wellington to be the name of a company which sells rubber boots, while that clever tea planter, Earl Grey, knows how to blend a decent brew.

It has been said that 'the past is a foreign country' – an observation possibly without argument; and in an age like now, the past would seem to pursue the present with the speed of a jet plane.

Technology, for example, moves at such a pace that the most sophisticated of computers can become virtually obsolete in the brief time it takes for it to be transported from factory to showroom; it becomes virtually history, then rapidly moves to oblivion.

Likewise, with those whom the modern media and entertainment worlds thrust into the spotlight of instant stardom; so often the lights dim and speedily they are banished from the memory of all but their most devoted fans. Fame, though, is but part of it; it has in a sense, a junior partner – indispensability.

There are in this world a goodly number of folk whom, while not especially well known beyond their community, are deemed essential to those around them. Ultimately such people will be congregated together – in graveyards; inevitable, of course – even the indispensable are not gifted with eternal life. Does the world as we know it grind to a halt with their demise?

No; others evolve to take over; in their lifetime they will have been assets, perhaps driving forces, but not irreplaceable. Missed and mourned, yes, but they never leave a void – the position will be filled. A further crop of 'indispensables' will be grown, until they in turn fall foul to the unrelenting scythe of 'the Grim Reaper'.

Such is this 'mortal coil'; it cannot be altered. It can, though, be anticipated if one adopts a pragmatic and realistic approach, bearing in mind the vagaries, inconsistencies and caprice of human beings – and their relatively short life span. In terms of elected office, this was brought home to me when told a tale regarding Jan Christian Smuts. This great South African statesman, admired and respected by his people and the wider world, had been an MP, in the same constituency, for some 60 years – in his country a legendary figure. In 1951, the great man, now well into his 80s, sought, once again, re-election; he was defeated. Stunned, almost heartbroken, he asked of his agent, 'Why have my supporters turned against me?' And the reply? 'They've not, Mr Smuts – it's just that too many are dead.'

And the moral of this tale? A simple one – all elected to public office, from Prime Minister to parish councillors, should 'jump before they are pushed'. Surely, thus, it has to be concluded that when it comes to fame and indispensability, the former is transitory, the latter, an illusion; the inference, reflected subtly in the film title, is correct – poor old 'What's 'is name' is in reality soon forgotten.

27

Funerals & Dress

*T*HE old dark suit used to hang, a touch forsaken, in a corner of the wardrobe.

It would be brought out for the occasional funeral and the even less frequent wedding, christening and other formal occasions. No longer is this so; in recent times it has been promoted to a more prominent position upon the clothes rail as it is required far more often than was the case a few years ago – the 'Grim Reaper's' ever more successful harvesting of my generation ensuring such brutal reality.

Fortunately, as I've gained no weight over the decades, it still fits tolerably well – or too well, if truth be told, due to the shrinkage of age (mine, not the suit's) there is room within for a sturdier body than mine. Now, in an era when the wearing of casual clothes is in vogue – some of it of a standard so shoddy no decent jumble sale would offer such – it is still no hardship to me, at happy events, to wear a competently tailored suit especially if complemented by a neat shirt and tie of tasteful, but rich colour (my wife, thankfully, usually does the choosing).

The problem is that in recent times those aforementioned formal celebratory occasions encouraging the donning of such attire – never that frequent – seem to come around about as often as Halley's Comet; modern social and cultural habits ensure, sadly one feels, celebrations to mark matrimony and birth become fewer, while other events which not long ago would encourage – possibly, almost demand – the wearing of formal dress are now dominated by casuality, the mode of dress reflecting this change in standards (lowering, some might say).

Funerals, though, are different – or predominantly so; there is a slight trend towards the sporting of bright colours (usually at the behest of the deceased's family), but the vast majority of such sad, and final, occasions still require, and receive, adherence to black; and as has been stated, the times, personally, when such sombre clothes need to be worn has moved from trickle to flood.

Mind you, while the donning of dark, formal attire is expected, it does not necessarily inhibit pursuit of fashion – not where ladies are concerned, anyway. In this direction, there are those who look as if they have just stepped out of a top London couturier; a majority, though, will dress smartly, but in the relatively functional clothes they have worn at previous sad times, while there will be those who will appear to have grabbed their funeral 'weeds' from the bin at the rear of a charity shop.

There will be, undoubtedly, greater uniformity in the garb used by men; dark suits, black shoes, white shirts (though several different shades) and black ties will abound. In this, though, while varying fashions will not be overt, standard of dress will. There will be those so

97

e

immaculate they could parade with The Coldstream Guards, others, while obeying the tradition of black, will look as if they have spent a sleepless night on a park bench, their clothes cursed with more creases than a score of cricket squares; and some of the suits will appear to have been in service since VE day and, often, no longer cover adequately the increasing bulk of the wearers.

Then – there are the ties. These vital tokens of mourning and respect will have immense – almost extraordinary – variation, some seeming to have originated in Savile Row, others from a council skip; there are those who will reach almost to the knees, others to the navel, while a number will be so short that they often appear to be strangling the wearer. They can be wider than a scarf or almost as narrow as a shoelace; some top quality; others bought in a charity shop or at a car boot sale, probably at one time the property of a member of the emergency services – a police officer or firefighter; also the degree of blackness will range from jet to a tired, murky dark grey. Many will look at ease in them, others, who view the donning of a tie on any occasion to be a restriction of liberty, distinctly uncomfortable.

There will be those, of course, close to the deceased whose grief and anguish will be such, they will be neither conscious or caring of their apparel. Nor should they be, in reality; for if ever there is an occasion when its cause is totally all that matters, it is a funeral, the bidding farewell to a colleague, a friend or a loved one. It is a woman or a man – or, even more sadly, a child – making an involuntary, coffin shrouded appearance prior to the dropping of the final curtain. How folk look is not really important – but being there is.

28

Enthusiasm – Good or Bad?

*T*HE eminent American writer and essayist, Ralph Waldo Emerson, once said that 'nothing great was ever achieved without enthusiasm.'

The Oxford Dictionary describes that dynamic word as being 'rapturous intensity of feeling for a person, cause, pursuit; passionate eagerness'. So, keeping this definition in mind, the words of this erudite academic are probably true; for no matter how much ability a person possesses, for them to move upwards towards the realms of major achievement could well require the leavening boost of 'passionate eagerness'. Also, the less gifted can certainly progress well beyond personal expectation with the addition of the driving positivity that is enthusiasm. Yet it could be argued there is a negative side to this seemingly admirable approach to life, especially when it becomes unbridled.

There was a gentleman – such a title is justified in description of this delightful chap – who was a member of a local council a few years ago: His enthusiasm was awesome. His fellow councillors were often submerged beneath a tsunami of ideas, projects and such like which this good man felt would benefit the community. Also, he would bring forward suggestions made by others, or which he had read in the paper, or seen on television and would generally push them forward with a joyful zeal which even the most single-minded evangelist would find hard to match. His proposals ranged from the useful to the preposterous, the feasible to the incomprehensible, the visionary to the pointless, the profound to the plain daft.

Meetings ran on as these brain waves were debated – often at great length – and then usually rejected as being fatuous, impractical or costing too much money. As with most serial enthusiasts, he expected others to share his passions and when he found such was not the case, he moved on – did not seek re-election, but took himself off to fresh ventures and projects (many), with some of which he remains involved.

Such introspective, single mindedness – which all too often accompanies relentless keenness – is one of its least attractive aspects. Folk doing charity work are sometimes offended when others do not wish to join them; those making street collections who expect passers-by to contribute no matter what the cause (not everybody wishes to donate towards, say, the setting up of a sanctuary for three legged horses in outer Mongolia); those who involve themselves in civic and community life in other ways – all should remember that rapture is a personal matter; one person's passion is another's poison.

For myself, even as a small boy I tended – possibly shamefully – to view life with suspicion rather than enthusiasm. If something looked promising or pleasurable, I tended to approach it looking for the loophole, rather than with an eagerness to enjoy or maximise the occasion.

The cynic's creed 'If it looks too good to be true then it probably is just that', still tends to lurk in the recesses of my perverse mind. Thus, in a long, chequered working life, I've always shied away from job ads which list 'enthusiasm' among the bevy of attributes the would-be employers are seeking in their applicants. It would be hypocritical not to do so.

I do question, though, why enthusiasm can be deemed so important. Nothing wrong with it, to a degree, but surely what is needed in a good employee is a sound work ethic, integrity, loyalty and, naturally, the required skills. Such, mind you, will also no doubt be expected by employers, from those possessed of the 'E' word; they, though, will enter their place of employment with an approach very different from more circumspect folk.

For they will hurtle into the working day with a 'passionate eagerness' that might well eschew foresight and a view of the wider picture – the 'fools rush in' syndrome. The more cautious, though, usually will approach matters in a different way. The upcoming hours of labour need to be eased into rather than hurtled towards. The route through the 'long (working) day's journey into night' must be planned with possible problems foreseen, and such vision is enhanced if one sits quietly for a while, simply contemplating. Did not the poet write 'what is this life if full of care, we have no time to stand (or sit) and stare?' Enthusiasts though, by their very nature, their innate eagerness, require constant action and involvement. To the more cerebral (or those seeking a quiet life), a touch of slothfulness can, at times, be a virtue – surely?

29

The 'Givers' in the World

*T*HERE is an old adage – 'Do all the good you can, by all the means you can, in all the ways you can, in all the places you can, to all the people you can, as long as ever you can.' – Noble and inspiring words and certainly a dictum to live by. They were written by one of the two famed brothers who founded the Methodist Church in the 18th century and made nonconformism a power in the land, especially here in the South West.

Charles Wesley, generally, wrote the hymns, so many still sung and enjoyed today, leaving most of the preaching to his dynamic sibling, John. Here, though, he articulated what people should do, the code that should guide them, whether Christian or not. Certainly a number of folk do follow such a path; there are dedicated members of all communities – though not nearly enough – who give so much of their time, energies, good will, on occasions money, to help those around them either directly or through charities and other organisations. They collect for causes, perhaps door-to-door or on bleak street corners; some serve in charity shops, or organise events. Many run marathons, swim or cycle long distances in pursuit of sponsorship money; folk adept artistically, create – paintings, pottery, garments, soft toys which they donate to charities, while others of culinary expertise bake delights, which again are sold for worthy causes.

There are too, numerous bodies of 'Friends'; hospitals, surgeries, cultural organisations, heritage, museums, the environment and so forth have such support from dedicated, focused groups who raise funds or give practical help; pursuers of positivity in a, so often, stubbornly negative world. We are blessed, also, with valiant bodies of men and women who regularly put themselves in harms way to help those in danger and distress.

Locally, the Dartmoor Rescue Group come to mind; they venture into some of the wildest terrain in Britain to find and snatch people from desperate situations whilst our rugged coasts are guarded by members of that admirable organisation, the Royal National Lifeboat Institution, brave folk who risk their lives to bring succour to those terrorised by the malevolent waters which often hammer our shores. No financial reward for them – no tangible personal gain of any kind. Thus day in, year out, thousands from all backgrounds are giving of their times, energies, goodwill, often money, to benefit the world about them. They are a crucial asset in the quest for fairness, happiness and the elevation of quality of life for us all; simply put, they are 'do gooders'.

Now to be described thus should be, surely, an accolade – indeed, a source of pride to be classed as one who concerns him, or herself with the problems or misfortunes of others, and seeks to alleviate them. After all, the opposite to citizens who try to improve the world – to do good in it – are those who desire to help nobody but themselves or, worse, those malevolents who treat others with contempt, possibly antagonism and aggression, even cruelty; such people are a minority but not rare. However, strangely and sadly, many such have their apologists – perhaps, perversely, even admirers, those who view such reprobates as being individuals exercising their perogative to be different.

Certainly in a free society people have the right to live their own lives; what nobody has, though, is the freedom to live beyond the law or to ignore the rights of others. If those who make, vitally, a positive contribution to our world are entitled 'do gooders' (who should be treasured), then this anti-social minority should be labelled 'do badders' – and shunned. In reality, this is rarely the case; the selfish, the greedy, the arrogant – even the evil – have their admirers and defenders. Adolf Hitler and Joseph Stalin retain followers; when the vicious Kray twins died, sizeable numbers of seemingly decent folk turned out for their funerals. Yet those devoting much time and effort towards improving the lives of others are often viewed with contempt – even hostility. From the lips of some, the words 'do gooders' are spat rather than spoken. Irrational? Certainly. Objectionable? Assuredly; but then as the northern saying goes 'there's nowt so queer as folk'. Fortunately most 'givers' in our communities seem to ignore such perversity; rather, they would appear content to live by the words of the comedian and radio presenter of the 1960s, 'cheerful' Charlie Chester. He always ended his popular broadcast with the words: 'Do good in the world and may it do you the world of good.'

30

The Devonshire Theory of Negativity

*I*T could be said that where Albert Einstein had his 'theory of relativity', Devonians are imbued with the philosophy of negativity – basically, large numbers of us are pessimistic in outlook. This could, to a degree, be due to the fact that we dwell in a large, predominantly rural county, with a majority of the population living outside of cities and large towns; thus the innate caution and reserve of the countryman and woman comes to the fore – especially amongst those native to the county.

Their view is that the sensible way to negotiate the obstacle course which is life is to hope for the best, but expect the worst. This somewhat jaundiced outlook is reflected in phraseology and habits which are still practised widely throughout the county – one based upon the feeling that negativity is the dominant force which guides our lives, possibly our destiny.

Prime examples of this were to be seen a few years back painted upon the walls of a local hostelry. The landlord, originally from 'up country', adapted rapidly to local, rural life and derived pleasure from the independence of word, thought and spirit of his collection of regulars, many of whom were farmers. He became so fascinated with the original, sometimes profound, occasionally daft comments they made, that he inscribed them on the walls of the bar for all to see.

A wide range of memorable, at times hilarious, quotes were included in this delightful 'library' so many marinated in a gloomy philosophy.

Possibly the pick of this captivating cluster was a question posed to 'mine host' by a weather beaten local son of the soil – 'yer boy, 'ee don't know nobody what don't want no 'ay do'ee?' When the enquiry is analysed it becomes apparent – though not easily – that the gent is asking, simply, if the landlord knows of anybody seeking to purchase hay. By posing the query in such a negative way, he is but assuming, pessimistically, that the man behind the bar will be unable to help him; he was correct.

Similar anticipation of failure was encompassed in an enquiry made to myself recently at my place of work; a fellow, clearly a Devon man, asked me (as I sat at my desk close to the technology section, merely 'watching the store', the experts at lunch) – 'yer, 'ee don't know nothing about computers do 'ee?' Once more this pessimistic assumption was accurate, even though the sign upon the door suggested the opposite, for he was confronted by, possibly, the daftest man in Britain in technical matters. Thus was I able to reassure him that, indeed, I am ignorant of them, totally. He went away somewhat mollified that his negative approach had been justified.

Then there was the lady who entered a local village post office (sadly, an ever rarer facility), enquiring of the post

The naturally pessimistic outlook of the Devonian.

mistress – 'I don't s'pose you sell stamps?' She was informed by the owner, with some acerbity (she had experienced a trying day), that seeing as 'post office' was inscribed over the premises in letters some two feet high, the deductive powers of 'Simple Simon' would be more than sufficient to reach the conclusion that the sale of stamps was amongst the services provided – or words to that effect.

Now, those of the 'glass half full' view of life might well argue such negativity can lead only to unhappiness amongst its devotees. Pessimists, though could well opine the opposite – such an approach to life could ensure the avoidance of discontent. For example, the farmer whose words were emblazoned on the pub wall was anticipating there would be no demand for his ' 'ay'; thus when such proved to be the case, he was only mildly dismayed. On the other hand, the publican might have said that he did know of a potential buyer for the dried grass; thus the purveyor would have covered the dual options admirably – if there was no buyer he would avoid the despondency or sense of failure over anticipation there might be, whilst if there was, it would prove a happy, pleasing surprise. Likewise with the computer and stamps; the potential customers did not expect their desires to be fulfilled, so their varying fortunes would have been accepted with aplomb.

That perceptive writer and poet, Rudyard Kipling, wrote that those with wisdom and strong character, could meet with triumph and disaster and 'treat those, two impostors just the same'. He would have been impressed at the great number of Devonians who, with, their shrewd adherence to negativity, live, to some extent, by that creed.

31

Local Councils – A Farewell

'GOODBYE To All That' was the title of the powerful, chilling memoirs of the eminent author and poet, Robert Graves, concerning the holocaust that was the 'Great War'.

This fine writer brought home the horrors, sacrifice, brutality plus the valiance and, often, nobility encompassed by those four devastating years during the second decade of the last century. However, quite apart from this being a mind concentrating book, it had a title of punch and clarity. Personally, there is no intention to write memoirs (which would bore folk to distraction), but should I ever do so, then I can think of no better title; but to what would I be saying adieu? Not yet to life, thankfully, but recently I waved a somewhat emotional farewell to four decades in public life – 42 years on the Tavistock Town Council, almost 32 on the West Devon Borough Council.

It all ended back in April and inevitably, one looks back. Mind you, it must be conceded immediately that sitting in a council chamber for all those years was surely massively less fraught, dangerous and terrifying than serving just 40 hours in the trenches; after all, death was never a threat – though possibly, terminal boredom could, occasionally, cast its shadow; also crucially, one could walk away from it without being shot for cowardice. I have now done just that, though it took a very long time to decide to do so. The people of Tavistock could, of course, have made the decision for me at elections every four years (every three when I started back in the 1970s).

A remarkable tolerance, generosity of spirit, and possibly, widespread amnesia, on their part – perhaps also to a degree, an adoption on the philosophy of sticking with the 'devil you know' – have seen me returned to office over the years, sent back to the chamber to continue a civic career of inactivity, negativity and procrastination. My gratitude to them knows no bounds, for unlike being sent to the trenches, I have been re-elected to an office, a way of life, plus community involvement, which I have enjoyed and found fulfilling.

Also, for a man who spends much of his life 'scribbling', yet possessing little imagination or original thought, council meetings and wider involvement with folk due to one's duties as an elected representative have provided material in abundance for the telling of tales. Certainly, over the years, I have heard spoken – also, it must be conceded, mouthed myself – words or statements truly crass, even plain daft. A debate, sometimes concerning 'vital' issues, but so often regarding a matter of relative triviality in the eyes of the electorate (for example, to decide the colour of new town hall curtains, or whether to give a grant of, say, £50 or £75 to some local organisation), can produce a myriad of comment – the witty, intense, hilarious, profound, silly, irrelevant, visionary, preposterous, wise, misguided, pedantic.

Indeed, discussion of these largely minor issues can be infinitely more protracted than that which concerns major matters and problems – pondering on the serious can certainly inhibit the flow of words. Then there are the electors; for decades I've been saved from solitude in the streets or local supermarkets and shops, folk stopping me, asking questions, airing views, 'venting spleens', grumbling, complaining, suggesting – at times, even praising. The widest range of subjects are traversed; usually it is something the council has done (or not done), but it can be a tirade against the Government (not guilty here) or concern on employment problems, even personal and marital ones (I skate around the latter). Often, mind you, it is centred on the 'soap opera' that is Plymouth Argyle; usually to that I make a full, but doom-laden contribution.

Whatever, these many years will, by me, be treasured. My dear wife and family have been central to my life; also my means of earning a living clearly vital; but the involvement with so many people over the decades has further enriched it. I've made a number of friends and it has to be said, a few enemies also – often implacable. To some, opposing their planning application would appear to stimulate greater malevolence than they would show towards a person running off with their spouse. So – would I do it all again? Yes, without any doubt. Will I miss it? Yes – at least for a while. Will I regret not standing for re-election? No – it was time to go; the world has moved on, but I have not; this 'old dog', now virtually toothless, is incapable of learning 'new tricks' even though some are better, by far, than those of yesteryear.

32

'Maid' & 'Boy'

A gentleman I know, a cynic, it has to be said, once opined to me regarding members of the female gender – and their accruing of years – 'you should never forget a lady's birthday but never remember her age'.

He maintained such a policy should be adopted towards any woman over-30 and most zealously in celebrating annual anniversaries involving a spouse or partner.

This, to be fair, could be said of some of the male sex also, those men to whom youth is so precious they spend decades mourning its passing. Strangely though, if gifted with real longevity, the outlook of both genders often does a complete about turn. When approaching their tenth decade, suddenly, with some, secrecy regarding their age turns to pride (possibly because they are outliving so many of their peers) and they trumpet to all and sundry that they were born when, say, Lloyd George was Prime Minister and Zeppelins roamed the skies. However, it must be conceded that coyness regarding age abounds amongst numerous ladies, and a goodly proportion of men.

So how does one neutralise in everyday outlook and

terminology, the inevitability of the mounting years (only one way to avoid such) – what descriptive words can be employed to give to the recipient the feeling that their birth certificate is fraudulently dated, that they are still in their prime?

Well, it could be argued that here in Devon we have used over the generations (and still do to an extent) two words which, when directed to those about us, allude subtly and gently to eternal youth – 'maid' when speaking to a lady, 'boy' when talking to a gent. The beauty of this brace of terms is that they can be used when speaking to all – whether nine or ninety, it is pertinent and acceptable; more, in fact, for they are warm, friendly expressions to which none, surely, can take offence.

There is, also, a second major benefit to their employment; for not only is the word acknowledgement of age by-passed, it is exceedingly useful if one is confronted by memory loss – or, amongst those of us of more advanced years, 'senior moments'. Suddenly face to face with someone with whom you are familiar but whose name has escaped into the ether, embarrassment and mental torture are avoided, with panache, if warmly one cries 'Hello maid (boy)', thus giving the impression that lady or gent is eternally in your thoughts.

Likewise if you do not know a person's moniker, but feel you should, or if confronted by someone to whom you are a familiar face, but whom to yourself is a stranger, then again the use, enthusiastically, of a welcoming phrase, ending with 'maid' or 'boy' can bring about instant rapport and good will; the frantic – and what would be all too apparent – highly confused search for a name could well provoke the opposite. These are simple modes of address, for most, if not all seasons.

Mind you, there are many other terms throughout this cosmopolitan land of ours used as alternatives to stating names. Some, such as 'love', 'dear', even 'sweetheart' and 'darling', are used widely; they have the plus of being gender blind, used for male and female alike – but are, it could be argued, somewhat too personal, too familiar. After all, to address someone as 'darling' could be seen as crossing the line dividing courtesy from something more intimate.

Like us here in the South West Peninsula, various regions throughout these isles have their own individual words used as terms of endearment, geniality or a sort of option when challenged with trying to remember a name. Many seem to look to the animal kingdom; in the Nottingham area, women – men also – are often addressed as 'me duck', whilst up in the North East ladies are hailed as 'pet'; the Scots use the term 'hen', one which it could be said has spread throughout the British Isles, as it is by no means unusual these days to see marauding bands of boisterous 'hens' making a night of it.

Words directed towards men proliferate – 'pal', 'mate', 'chum', 'squire', 'guvnor' are examples; the problem, though, is that the first three imply friendship – often where none exists – whilst the latter pair speak of deference rather than comradeship.

No, 'maid' and 'boy' are surely better in that they are gentle, friendly and democratic; the Devonshire dialect also – thoughtfully – provides a back up term should there be any doubts over a person's gender; they would be addressed as, 'me 'andsome'.

33

The 'I' Word

*T*HERE are a few words in the English language which are often referred to in the media by their first letter.

To the fore of these is the four digit 'F' word, while not far behind is another of similar length commencing with 'S'. I have to admit that on occasions I utter a six letter one, starting with 'B', usually round about five o'clock of a Saturday afternoon having just suffered the football results.

These utterances are, of course, oaths and, it must be conceded, tend to proliferate. There is, though, a further word which, although perfectly legitimate and respectable, dominates, seemingly, the air waves and television screens to an alarming extent – the 'I' word.

An adjective, it consists of four syllables and contains ten letters. It is heard incessantly, no matter what the subject, the occasion, the mood; sometimes 'ly' is added to move it from adjective to adverb, which, again, is heard with monotonous, mind-numbing frequency. Now this would be understandable, possibly, if there were few alternatives. Assuredly, however, such is not the case, for a glance at a thesaurus will show there are upwards of 20 words which could be employed in its place. These range from absurd to unbelievable, astounding to inconceivable, exceptional to marvellous, amazing to wonderful, fantastic to preposterous, plus many others, including, simply, 'great'.

And the 'I' word so used, and brutally abused? 'Incredible'; to be fair, while in everyday conversation it is spoken too often, that is still relatively minimal compared to its confetti like proliferation from the lips of broadcasters. To put this into some context it would be helpful to quote the dictionary text regarding the meaning of the word; the Oxford English describes 'incredible' as being, 'that which cannot be believed – amazing'. Thus it is a term which should be directed at describing the extraordinary, the impossible, the implausible – perhaps even the bizarre; yet it is employed relentlessly in manifold directions, mouthed to enhance the relatively commonplace, used so often it ceases to extol the truly remarkable.

Good GCSE results (nothing unusual) will be classified as 'incredible', someone living to an advanced age, likewise, as will folk doing, achieving, or attempting that which is merely laudable or interesting; the grower of the largest or heaviest marrow at the local produce show might, by some, be credited with doing something 'incredible'.

A warm day is classed as being 'incredibly' hot, a nippy one, likewise cold. Little, in the eyes of the media, would appear to be permitted to be ordinary; issues cannot be of moderate relevance or importance – nor emotions and achievements. This 'I' word permeates present day descriptive talk so comprehensively that it pollutes and indeed, is most detrimental to our fine language. Also, arguably of even greater consequence, a meaningful, imaginative term describing the extraordinary has been so neutralised it is now difficult to use in connection with those matters, those occurrences and attainments which actually do fall within the narrow confines of 'that which cannot be believed – amazing'.

Migratory birds that fly thousands of miles across the oceans to return to the same nests in spring; men and women who overcome disability, illness, pain to achieve for others as well as themselves; soldiers on the battlefield, folk in everyday life, who perform acts of heroism without thought for their own safety; those who stand firm for their rights and beliefs – and for those of others – against brutal, oppressive regimes, risking prison, torture, often death in the process; is not the 'I' word, used in its correct sense, a fair, meaningful way to describe such attainment?

Now, some people might well feel it is a touch foolish to be upset over and rail against the misuse of a solitary word; one, possibly, can sympathise with such a view. This ten letter term though, is not a prosaic one, not one to be mouthed lightly; it is meant to express the extraordinary – the amazing – but now is cheapened in lamentable fashion, employed tsunami-like in everyday speech by those too lazy – or unprofessional – to select from numerous, more appropriate alternatives.

The English language is magnificent. It is the written word of Shakespeare and Dickens, that spoken so inspirationally by the likes of Winston Churchill and Martin Luther King.

As is said of rural post offices – 'use it or lose it'.

34

Matrimony

*T*HE late Mickey Rooney was clearly much better at finding spouses than retaining them; for the well known, long living Hollywood star, was married no fewer than eight times.

Clearly this was not the kind of record with which anybody could be happy – and assuredly not proud – but the diminutive actor did deliver one of the all time classic lines regarding matrimony, one richly marinaded in both cynicism and wit. He said he had always wed early in the morning so that if the marriage did not work out then at least he had 'not wasted the entire day'.

There is, though, in a sense, a happy ending to this, as his final union, to the lady who is now his widow, lasted longer than all the others added together.

Matrimony has been going for a very long time and naturally attracts much comment and observation, much of it, inevitably, of a cynical nature. An old school friend of mine, back in our youth, opined that 'it is a most unnatural relationship'. However, he clearly managed to adapt to such, as his wife and he recently celebrated their ruby wedding anniversary.

Another comment which would come on occasions from the lips of some fellows was that the problem of wedlock was it meant that one man was keeping another's daughter. It was always a self indulgent, 'clever dick' line which withered under scrutiny; for this 'other gent's daughter', generally, is the spine of the union, running the home, bringing up the children, often going out to work – the hub, the crucial figure in a good, happy family.

In this slightly more enlightened age, it is the sort of pseudo macho comment rarely heard. Indeed, if common sense and observation were not sufficient to debunk such nonsense, then statistics surely should. After all, if all these wives are enjoying the luxury of being kept by a man, then why is it that most divorces are sought by women? Mind you, it could also be down to an odd view I heard, many years ago, voiced by a marriage guidance 'expert' on the radio; she said that as a general principle a woman should love a man 'because of his faults – not despite them'. It struck me then, as now, as being strange advice; after all, some fellows have defects which it must be difficult indeed, sometimes impossible – to live.

Still, it is most probable the upcoming years will see a decline in the divorce rate in this country. This, though, will not be down to an upsurge of tolerance between couples – rather it will be dictated by simple mathematics. The fact is that fewer folk, year on year, are marrying. Increasing numbers of the population – of wide ranging age – do not take on spouses; they go into partnerships, living together (often on a reasonably permanent basis), without making a legal or religious commitment to each other.

Years ago, those sharing their lives in such a way would have been deemed to have entered in to a 'common law' union, a phrase now rarely heard. Whatever the term, numerous homes now are shared by, and children born to, men and women living together (indeed, same gender couples also) their adherence to each other, and where relevant to their offspring, strong and enduring. Yet, to a man of my generation, the description partner, does not gel as well as it might; do not solicitors and business people have partners? Bridge players, likewise? Not that a word can matter that much, but the reality which lies behind it possibly does; after all, if people really are committed to each other, love each other, and wish to share, in theory at least, their lives until the 'grim reaper' comes to call, then why not make that a commitment in a legal sense; why not take vows? Folk, dearly, would still be able to walk away from them – but importantly not easily, not capriciously, not without much thought and consideration. Still, it is a free society.

What is crucial is love. I once knew an elderly gent who devoted his life to the care of his disabled wife – totally. One day I complimented him upon it; his response – 'but my dear chap, it is my privilege.' That is love!

35

Amateur Weather Forecasters

*T*HE coming of spring brings to our notice two distinct species of wildlife rarely heard except during the second quarter of the year. The later arrival, usually, is the cuckoo, who 'comes in April, sings his song in May, changes his tune in the middle of June, and July, flies away' (presumably this applies to the female also of this parasitic bird); why it departs then is not apparent to most of us – perhaps it is to avoid the bulk of the tourists or the start of the new football season. Generally, however, this winged, temporary immigrant is preceded by a creature native to these shores, rarely actually seen at any time, but noisy through to mid-summer – the amateur weather forecaster.

Now why, so often, he is listened to with greater trust and confidence than is his professional counterpart who nests in the Met Office – based here in Devon – is one of life's mysteries (and it only ever seems to be a he; perhaps there is no female of the breed, which beggars the question as to how they procreate). The professional of the species, however, seems to have as many of the distaff gender as

f

the opposite which, in a society seeking fairness, is re-assuring – all too often mere lip service is paid to the concept of equal opportunities for women. These qualified scientists – for that is what they are – also have the most advanced, sophisticated assistance towards making their forecasts, both short and long term. Despite this, though, they err, generally, on the side of caution when it comes to predicting that which the elements have in store for us, rarely going beyond a couple of weeks, maximum.

Looking ahead just this shortish time, they will not talk with certainty, even though their aids regarding assessing weather to come are comprehensive – coastal stations, satellites, balloons and so forth – the most modern gear the world can provide. Thus it must, amongst these knowledgeable people, be frustrating, mystifying, indeed infuriating, that their scientifically based assessments of weather to come are often treated with suspicion, whilst those from the mouths of total amateurs are, by some, accorded a remarkable level of trust, and respect; and such soothsaying often concerns the long term – many months ahead.

Late spring and summer are the seasons towards which their confident predictions are directed – May to September. After this, one can only assume that, possibly, they migrate, though it is more likely they hibernate, a sleep from which they awake come the spring equinox in late March. Then, following a brief period when they formulate their sooths, they pronounce them to the nation – well, to those awaiting their visions, anyway.

It is probable fewer in major towns and cities take notice, but here in the rural South West, with our

"Flamingoes on the beach – sure to be a hot summer!"

proximity to open landscape and nature, plus our more traditional outlook and ways, a sizeable measure of credence is accorded these meteorological mystics. Now, if a goodly majority of these pundits said roughly the same thing, then even the most cynical would have to grant respect – albeit possibly grudgingly – to their visions of what is to come from the sky during the months ahead. This, though, is rarely the case; one forecaster might well say that flamingoes (rumoured) have been seen on a Devon beach, this pointing to a hot summer. Another will pronounce the opposite – a cold spell right through to autumn is on the cards due to the fact, say, that hyacinths flowered late; 'wrong' will opine some other weather expert – a wet summer approaches down to the fact the wind was in the west on April Fool's Day and full moon fell on a Friday.

Mind you, why we as a race are preoccupied with the upcoming elements is not hard to discern; after all, if one lives in Saudi Arabia, or perhaps, the Amazon rain forest, 'the little grey cells' are not going to be taxed forecasting a few months ahead; for they have constant 'climate'. We British, though, endure 'weather' – perhaps more capricious than any other on Earth.

Personally, my confidence in the professionals' ability to give a forecast of just tolerable accuracy is not high – in the amateurs' ability, nil.

Members of Parliament

ALMOST certainly it puts me into a minority, but I am someone who has, generally, confidence in and respect for Members of Parliament.

True there are amongst them rogues (though surely far fewer than is widely believed), plus a number who see the position as being the gateway to power and prestige; also a few who relish the title and status, but do not represent the people as well as they should. The majority though, I firmly believe to be honest, honourable men and women who work diligently and constantly for the people they represent and do it for a salary possibly less than that of a headteacher of a modestly sized primary school and assuredly less than that paid to the average GP. The Prime Minister's annual stipend is less than many a premier league footballer receives weekly, whilst a cabinet minister's remuneration can be less than that paid to a senior officer in a district council.

Granted, expenses are generous and, as is so very well known, open to abuse; but the fact remains that a Member of Parliament is not rewarded over generously for his or her labours – and has very limited job security. For within five years MPs have to apply to have their contracts renewed with absolutely no guarantee of success. If one is the Labour member for the likes of Ebbw Vale or the Conservative occupant of the ultra safe seat of, say, Kensington then such fortunate folk are not going to be over stressed awaiting their results on election night and their performances as representatives of the people over the period of the parliament will have little relevance (not a good situation).

On the other hand, there are many occupying, uneasily, constituencies where they have small majorities, their future prospects totally at the whim of a somewhat capricious electorate; their frustration here – and vulnerability – is the fact that so often their performance as the elected member for the area, no matter how good it has been, no matter how hard, honestly and unrelentingly they have worked, will have little bearing on their future job prospects. They could well have been magnificent in the role, but it will avail them little if they sport the colours of a party out of favour in the land.

There they will stand in the early hours of, probably, a May morning with a returning officer announcing voting figures which could well mean instant dismissal from the job they have done so ably and diligently for the past five years. No appeal here; no suing against wrongful dismissal; no prospect of the 'boss' having a change of mind and offering a new contract; the P45 will be in the post, a first class stamp attached and the hapless politician who was in high profile, influential, fulfilling employment on the Thursday will find him or herself in the job centre the following day (in theory at least).

It must make the situation even harder for them to bear, to know all too well that sympathy for their 'plight' will hover between minimal and nought. Yet, as 'public sector workers' (which they are, their salaries coming from taxes and government), do they not have a right to expect at least the same sympathy which would come the way of others employed by the state? If a teacher, nurse, police officer, firefighter, council worker, civil servant, or the like, is made redundant there will be many, even now in our somewhat cynical, rather selfish society, voicing concern over their plight even though in most instances they will receive reasonable redundancy and severance payments, plus, often, good pensions. Also a majority will probably have a trade union fighting for their rights and their futures.

The poor old ex MPs, however, are on their own. Many mind you, have professions to go back to (lawyers, doctors and the like) whilst others will quite possibly have made productive 'contacts' during their time in the Palace of Westminster, perhaps will have done favours (quite legitimate ones) that might prove to have been 'bread cast upon the water' which can float back as loaves of opportunity in their hour of need. Mind you, despite its uncertainties, its vulnerability to the mood of the people, a goodly number of those displaced will, come the next election, still seek a return to the green benches of the House of Commons.

Personally I've never had either the ambition or, assuredly, the ability to be an MP; however, I've always felt there would be something attractive – certainly comfortably rewarding, interesting and stress free – in being the member for a very safe seat here in the South West representing a party permanently in opposition.

37

Alcohol

$\mathcal{A}$MONGST many other memorable melodies, that sublime crooner, Dean Martin, sang 'Little Old Wine Drinking Me'. Now it could be that the famous American performer did, indeed, imbibe a fair share of the juice of the grape, but it is for the consumption of whisky and bourbon he is best remembered apart, of course, for that smooth, velvet like tenor voice.

How it affected his health I know not – he lived a quite reasonably long life – but it certainly was part of his persona, even perhaps a trademark, in that he often went on stage carrying a glass containing ample portions of the 'amber nectar' (and it wasn't lager). Between warbling his memorable offerings, he would take a sip or two; which leads to the recounting of a priceless response he once made to a lady in the audience who accused him of being inebriated (a touch unlikely as he was so very professional). Apparently he looked at her, shook his head, smiled, and said in respectful tones 'Ma'am, you're not drunk as long as you can lie on the floor without holding on.' Sadly, in this binge drinking age (though, mercifully, it is reported to be on the decline) there are all too many folk – usually young – who spend far too much of their time lying on floors, or roads, greatly the worse for wear, even if they do not have to 'hold on'.

Still, it has to be said that whilst alcohol – due perhaps to it being relatively cheap, more easily accessible, and people, generally, being better off – is consumed more widely and heavily than during the days of my youth, I would be guilty of, at best, amnesia, at worst, a blatant refusal to confront reality, if I were to suggest that back then the imbibing of liquor was not an important part of so many people's lives, including my own. Indeed, it ever has been, right back to the dawn of history – did not Jesus turn water into wine for the benefit of guests at a wedding?

Some 50 years back, mind you, there were far fewer places where one could purchase beer and spirits (wine, then, was rarely consumed). There were few supermarkets, whilst ordinary shops usually found it very difficult to get a licence to sell alcohol; pubs provided the vast bulk of drink, and they were then constrained by strict regulations regarding opening hours, especially on a Sunday.

Despite this, there was always plenty for the drinking man or woman to consume; draught beers dominated, such as bitter and mild (few lagers) although the likes of brown and light ales, plus stout, often were bottled. Spirits such as whisky, rum and gin wetted many a glass, though vodka was far less common.

The products of vineyards were also rare, unlike the harvest from local apple orchards which was to be found in pubs and a multitude of farms; 'Scrumpy' was the liquid produced when crushing the apples – technically, it was cider, but probably bore about as much resemblance to present day brews as does clotted cream to skimmed milk. For this was Westcountry 'moonshine', a pint of which would assault the senses of anyone not used to it, a quart of which would make them stagger to their beds.

Even back then some hostelries would not stock it, aware that its potency could lead, all too often, to aggression in many, even some quite used to it. Great numbers of farms though, kept barrels of the greenish, brownish fermented juice, many brewing it themselves. Mainly they made it for their own use, but often would give some to their friends and neighbours, or make a few bob in selling it. Though farmers with an orchard, my parents did not make scrumpy, preferring to sell off the apples; there was always a jar or two of it in the house, however, though rarely touched by myself even when a young man. Shamefully, I must admit, proud Devonian though I am, to not really liking scrumpy. I did enjoy beer, though – brown ale, mainly – and spent far too much of my early years in licensed premises. Still, in an era of probably greater individuality – and eccentricity – one did meet folk who linger in the memory for various reasons, including their drinking preferences.

One fellow drank only whisky with a dash of milk, another a mixture of gin and rum; an old farmer, pints of scrumpy with a double scotch added to 'give it a bit of character', as he used to put it. For good or ill, they don't make them like that anymore. Some, also, would drive home afterwards in those pre-breathalyser times. Different days, indeed.

38

Come the Revolution

*T*HERE is a phrase heard occasionally – and down the years – when someone is dissatisfied with life in general, and governments and officialdom in particular; all will be put right, 'Come the Revolution.'

The reality, though, is that whilst so many countries have, over the centuries had vicious, devastating internecine conflicts – many bloody in the extreme – such barbarities, generally, have not afflicted us.

The French, Russians and other European states have had traumatic, murderous upheavals during their histories (some recent); Central and South America, post colonial Africa, many Asian states, have had, and still endure, periods of, at best, chronic instability, at worse, anarchy and carnage. Across the Middle East there is brutal internal blood letting, citizens fighting dictators and governments (so many corrupt); folk butchering one another.

Here, though, in our thousand plus year's history, such has never really taken place. We had a civil war, true, back in the 17th century – assuredly a violent time – but this was basically a struggle by Parliament to establish their democratic right to rule rather than accepting matters be left in the hands of a monarch determined to govern according to his or her personal whim. Later that century, there was the bloodless 'Glorious Revolution', when Protestants William of Orange and Mary Stuart, ousted Catholic James II – by will of people and Parliament alike – with a minimum of fuss or inconvenience to anybody, except James, of course.

Probably the nearest England has ever come to real revolution was back in the 14th century – 'the Peasant's Revolt'. This, though, rapidly lost its considerable initial momentum; the duplicitous behaviour of the young King Richard II could be partly responsible for this, taking the sting out of the uprising by seeming to accede to most of the rebels' demands, then, when the peasant 'army' were off their guard thinking they had triumphed, having their leaders seized and executed; then followed the scattering of the demoralised, oppressed peasants by the king's troops. Mind you, it did him little good in the long run as he himself met a violent early death. However, the relative ease with which Richard earned the upper hand, almost 700 years ago, showed that even then there was no great stomach for revolution; those who stormed the Bastille, or arose in Russia in 1917, would not have been appeased with promises.

No, we British are essentially believers in evolution, not revolution. Rather than take to the streets, we prefer to nip to the polling booth every five years (though sadly, many folk don't even bother to do that), go off to the supermarket then turn on the television the next morning to see whom the Queen will be inviting to form the next government; all very ordered, seemly and civilised – far better than pursuing the murderous mayhem of revolution.

Anyway, such strife would assuredly play havoc with property values and interfere with holidays. Our aversion to taking to the streets and toppling governments by using violence rather than the vote (though, in reality, such an avenue of democratic expression has only been in place in any meaningful way for the past 150 years, or so), has to be down, surely, to character traits peculiar to our race.

British phlegm, tolerance, our natural personal reserve – possibly even insularity – plus a generosity of spirit, and patience, which at times can be taken advantage of, are possibly major reasons for our avoidance of internal, anarchic conflict; but does not another aspect of life here play a role – the elements? It is said that where other countries have climate, the British suffer 'weather'. The angry of South America, Africa, Asia, the Middle East, even France in July, can be, and long have been, fairly sure that on the vast majority of days 'the sun will have his hat on'. Also, its heat will incubate dissent and encourage the disaffected (also the lawless) to take to the streets, confronting the forces of the state – or enemy, as many would see it.

A different situation exists here; whether January or June, weather is no more predictable than football results – though rain during the latter month could be a touch warmer.

Whatever, it would not help the cause to have to charge the forces of 'oppression' with a weapon in one hand and an umbrella in the other and if the sun did shine, the pragmatic citizens of this country would probably feel one had to take advantage of it – and thus make for the beaches rather than breach the barricades.

39

Board Games – A Curse?

$\int$T is a fair bet that back in the spring there were folk sitting in secluded offices planning mayhem – perhaps even a form of mental torture – for the Yuletide. Come summer, their creations would probably be in the process of manufacture prior to being packaged (usually in ridiculously large boxes when considering the often minimal contents), then sent off to shops where they will be displayed alongside a price tag akin to the cost of filling a small car with petrol; and in these retail outlets, with autumn approaching, they are now appearing like unwanted guests at a wedding.

Having said all this, astonishingly to me, they do appear to be desirable to numerous folk, as there is always a buoyant market for this manifold collection of misery. I refer to board games, for which, I must concede, I possess, and ever have done, feelings which meander from dislike to loathing, frustration to boredom; incomprehension to total bewilderment.

Even as a small child I could raise no enthusiasm towards them. Back then, mind you, there were few – just the likes of Ludo, Snakes and Ladders (better than most because it requires no real skill) and Monopoly (far too complicated and decision requiring for me). Even at this early age I became aware that I possessed the attention span of a goldfish, powers of perception less than that of the average gerbil, the deductive abilities of a mollusc plus a deplorably low competitive edge – and absolutely no patience at all. Board games held no allure then, have not since, and never will now.

Not that I've always been able to avoid them; over the years, firstly children, then grandchildren have caught me in moments of weakness or distraction and trapped me into playing the like – some of them bemusingly obscure – at which I have always been trounced. That they knew, and know, I am perpetual 'cannon fodder' in the warfare of family competitions has, without doubt, made me the ideal participant in these ordeals. Indeed, if ever beaten by me at anything of this nature it would be a blow to them of such devastation that counselling would be required.

At 'Cluedo', I'm clueless – I'd not ascertain the murderer even if one of the suspects came to life and confessed; although I spend much of my time with a pen in my hand, at word games I'm inept, and not to finish last in, say, 'Scrabble', would be for me a moment of triumph – and shame for whomever did. Of course, the number of such tortures increases yearly – which brings us back to those devious people and their fiendish creations that infest the shelves of shops and stores throughout the land. Not only are they burdening a hapless population with puzzles more obscure than Egyptian hieroglyphics, more mind concentrating than the theories of Einstein and

Euclid, more boring than watching grass grow, surely also they can bring grief. For on Christmas morning, people of all ages will awaken anticipating, often excitedly, the delights which will come their way during this magical day, either from Santa himself, or found wrapped in shimmering paper laying beneath the Yuletide tree; youngsters will possibly be hoping for the latest sophisticated toy, perhaps computer games and the like, even the latest mobile phone (already obsolete by the time they receive it, so rapid is technological advancement); whilst their seniors might well, if female, eye that enticing looking gift hoping for, perhaps, a tasteful, fashionable and desirable creation, and those of the male gender, might hope that gaily hued parcel will contain a trendy item of clothing, or a useful gadget for workshop or car.

Then comes the moment of truth – the seductive looking present is opened; the jollity and bonhomie of the festive season fades into the background; sobriety (disastrous at Christmas) and seriousness reigns. For there it lies, a box containing the complex, possibly incomprehensible – assuredly frustrating and, to many, pointless – game. Instructions will be printed in a dozen or so languages, with English being little more meaningful than the rest; the board will be laid out, along with such as perhaps counters, dice and other paraphernalia – with slowly, painstakingly, the hope being that somewhere along the line somebody will suss out how to play it. The 'Queen's Speech' will be compulsory viewing for even the most ardent republican, in the hope that by the time it has finished, the wretched game will have self combusted. No chance, of course; and no prospect of having them banned. Looking on the bright side, unlike a tax return, participation is still not compulsory; it can, though, be hard to avoid.

40

Local Football –
The Golden Days

*D*ANNY Blanchflower, that gifted footballer and raconteur of the 1950s and 60s, used to tell an amusing, perceptive tale regarding his boyhood days in Belfast; it concerned football 'kickabouts' in the, then, mainly traffic free streets and the selection of teams from the motley bunch of youngsters keen to pound the cobbles in pursuit of an ancient tennis ball.

According to Danny, those designated by their peers as the best two players would select their rival sides. The process followed, generally, the application of a seemingly sound, though arguably unkind logic; the speedy lad went on one wing, the small one on the other, the big fellow went centre forward, the fat chap centre half – and the idiot played in goal.

I've always claimed the reason I spent my chequered, grossly under-achieving football career as 'custodian' was not due to this but, rather – unlike these days – as a lad and young man I carried somewhat more weight than was wise, sufficient to ensure my pace was that of a lethargic snail. Still, the epithet 'idiot' was probably quite accurate;

138

anyone with just a modicum of sense would have assessed his own dearth of talent and would have retired from the game in his teens or possibly played outfield; to be fair, in this direction I was probably even worse than in goal.

It was, though, relatively stress free; for as my incompetence was matched, almost, by that of some in front of me, few of the many sides I played for ever took to the field with any expectation of victory. There was a plus, too, for even on the coldest day, so busy would I be trying – usually with an embarrassing lack of success – to repel mud-caked footballs, that hypothermia was never a threat, nor boredom. Astonishingly, despite conceding, regularly, a deluge of goals, I did on occasions receive praise. The most noteworthy was upon my debut for a local village side on a foul day in January; I was about 17. Pensilva were the opposition, a good side who, at that time, played on a pitch with a slope only marginally less than the north side of the Eiger. Playing down the incline in the first half we were only losing 3-0; the second half, though, it was as if we were confronting the Chinese army, with 90 per cent of the action taking place in our penalty area.

A further half dozen goals were conceded – which didn't fill me with any satisfaction; in fact, the sole save I recall making was when the ball hit me in the face and diverted up and over the bar. The manager, though, saw it in a far more positive light – bless him. As we came off the pitch he bounded over, thumped me on the back and uttered words I've never forgotten: 'Well done, boy; if it hadn't been for you, we'd have had a hammering.'

A week later I was able to understand his delight; we lost 15-0 – truly a thumping.

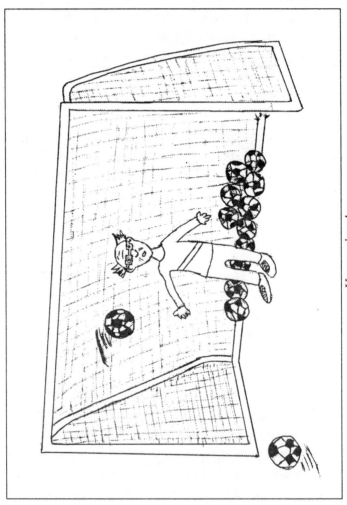

Happy days!

My football career was sporadic and spent playing mainly for village sides in the West Devon area. I did move about quite a bit as my general ineptitude meant I fell into the 'Don't phone us we'll phone you' category. Assuredly there was no great number seeking my signature on 'transfer deadline day'.

The division in which most local teams played was the Tavistock section of the Plymouth Combination League. Drawn from West Devon and the Tamar Valley, the proximity of these outfits meant that rivalry was fierce; no quarter given or asked; no prisoners taken. Most of the players then resided in the villages for which they played – as often had generations of their family. Pride was involved, sometimes long running feuds, while referees allowed a level of physicality (sometimes, almost brutality) which would never be tolerated today. Indeed, I remember complaining to the 'man in black' on one occasion when a lumbering opponent had jumped on my head as I lay on the ground.

'It's a man's game, boy,' said the official.

Yet the final whistle usually brought peace and a fraternising with 'the enemy' in the nearest pub – the players often unwashed. For changing and ablution facilities were, at best, spartan, all too often non existent, many clubs relying on God to provide the 'showers' – often with hailstones thrown in. Still, the caked mud and blood kept the limbs warm – important in an age when central heating, even in hostelries, consisted of a few logs flickering forlornly in a grate. Happy days? Yes. Would I like to go back to them? No – a quiet, sedentary life holds far more allure these days.

41

Room 101

*D*URING the past century there will have been few more perceptive, visionary writers than George Orwell. His works so often seemed to expose the weakness – at times sheer folly – of blind idealism.

He, like many others in the 1930s, went to join the 'International Brigade' who rushed to the aid of the democratically elected socialist government of Spain, threatened by the fascist rebel army of General Franco.

Many since have written and spoken of the sacrifices and nobility of those rallying to the cause, often dying for it. In *Homage to Catalonia*, Orwell, whilst acknowledging such, illustrates the incompetence, ill-discipline and poor leadership from government down and, at times, the sheer stupidity which gifted victory to Franco.

In what is arguably his masterpiece, *Animal Farm*, he shows with chilling clarity how in terms of equality and equity, 'idealism' can, rapidly, become 'Stalinism'. Then there is that which is probably his most famous work, *1984*, a disturbing tale of the ultimate totalitarian state. In the story, those who offend the powers that be are confined within 'Room 101' to be confronted with that which they hate – or which terrifies them most; in the case of the central character in the book, Winston Smith, it is rats (with which I can empathise).

Over the years, however, Room 101 has become as well known as the book itself and in recent times television programmes have come along with personalities saying what, or whom, they dislike (sometimes hate) sufficiently to see such consigned to the oblivion of this room, usually to a maximum of three.

Personally I would find it impossible to restrict my selection to just a trio – if let loose I would probably fill the Albert Hall with the articles, customs, ideas and folk that in my prejudiced, perhaps bigoted way, I feel would not be missed – well, certainly not by me.

Barbecues, assuredly, would be cast into this room of horror – both the appliances and the events. The joy of sitting in a garden in our uncertain weather, trying to hold a glass in one hand, a plate in another whilst eating, presumably, using a third has ever eluded me; and the food itself can often be little short of dire – poorly cooked meat, burgers and sausages wrapped in crumbly bread rolls, grease oozing onto hands, possibly clothes, flies and midges causing mayhem; no, a session at the dentist holds more allure. So often this grim fare is created by men that would not be seen within a mile of the pristine cooker in their modern kitchen, but are delighted to stand before a primitive cooking device in an, often, rain soaked garden shrouded by smoke and fumes.

Also incarcerated will be excessively paid sports' summarisers and pundits who clutter the television screens in absurd numbers, ensuring widespread pressing of the 'mute button', along with the horde of 'celebrities', of whom few would have ever heard, that tend to dominate the media even though, often, they display little evidence of ability; they will be in the company of those public sector workers who appear to believe they have a divine right to retire years – decades, sometimes – and on far larger pensions, than the vast majority in the private sector.

Space will be found for pubs and restaurants (usually the former) who claim 'to be passionate about food', serving only 'locally sourced' meat, veg and so on, yet produce overpriced meals of mediocrity using ingredients from far beyond the shores of our islands, often warmed up in a microwave.

Television licences would be cast into the room (it's time the BBC funded itself) along with the vast majority of TV comedians (just not funny).

That American promoted – if not created – abomination 'Hallowe'en' would be amongst the first banished, along with the motley collection who spend so much of their time – and annoy many of the rest of us – doing impressions of the long gone Elvis Presley.

The mind numbingly boring curse of 'reality television' would follow, along with *Strictly Come Dancing* (although that could be reprieved if the inane hype was eliminated and meaningful time was given to the dancing itself).

Christmas would be spared, but anyone espousing sentimentality regarding Dickensian and Victorian Yuletides would be incarcerated instantly – the glorifying of an era when the majority of people lived in poverty and would have experienced a miserable festive period is almost offensive.

There are other goods, people, events, customs and so forth which this jaundiced scribe would thrust into 'Room 101' but as to list them would fill the rest of this newspaper, no more will be mentioned – for now.

g

42

Councillors – Media Stars?

WHEN I look back over the decades, I realise that when confronted with decisions – and such are the punctuation marks of life – I have made vastly more bad, sometimes calamitous, than good. In the area of employment – especially in my earlier years – I changed jobs with such regularity that often on a Monday morning I'd not be certain where I was heading.

Two vital matters, though, I did get right – one a very long time ago – the other recently. That of the past took place in the early 1970s when I asked Ann to marry me, and she agreed; whether or not she feels it was one of her better decisions is another matter; a lady of loyalty and tolerance, she has never said. The second was enacted just a few months back when I retired from public life, choosing not to seek re-election to either the Tavistock Town or West Devon Borough Councils after many years on both. My reasons were manifold, but to the fore was the desire 'to jump before being pushed' – and seeing some of the shocks regarding borough elections, I am glad I did.

Recently, though, a story on the front page of the *Times*

convinced me my stepping down was, on my part, an exceedingly rare act of wisdom and, in truth, good fortune. The headline appeared positive – 'Leading the Way'; admirable, as long as the path leads in the right direction, and others are doing the navigating (I would not like to pursue any trail where I took the lead). However, after reading just a few sentences, a chill of Arctic proportions afflicted my spine. The story concerned the laudable efforts of the town council to enhance its accountability; in the third paragraph it stated that £10,000 was to be invested in a brand new broadcasting system for the chamber which (terrifying words, these) 'will enable people to watch and listen to the debates and decisions made.'

Thus, the arcane practices of local democracy on view to all following a mere flick of a switch; folk will be able to sit by their firesides of an evening and witness the efforts of their local representatives. In principle there is dearly nothing wrong with this; everyone has the right to see how council tax is spent, and the performance of those they have elected.

Up until now, though, people would have to take themselves off to the council chamber, sit on hard chairs – frequently in the cold – in order to absorb proceedings which often have the pulsating vibrancy of watching grass grow. Thus attendance has generally been sparse, folk only turning up in numbers when the council has done something to invoke their wrath (a major hike in the 'rates' can usually accomplish this); and those who do come along rarely stay long, the relative discomfort of their surroundings overcoming their zeal to witness living democracy. Usually only our excellent journalists remain to relate in the local press that which is decided by committees – an invaluable service to councillors as well as electors, there being times when I would study the report to find out what decision, after convoluted, obscure debate, we had arrived at. What would not be relevant to the report, thus not stated, would be the gamut of outlooks and eccentricities possessed by councillors (as is the way with all groups of human beings); their foibles, biases, intolerances, faux pas, would be witnessed only by a few.

Those halcyon days for the town council would appear to be gone; one fears that this honourable, honest, hard working body, in splendid pursuit of the spirit of transparency, have possibly opened themselves up to negative, cynical scrutiny, the kind which entices folk, at leisure, to watch such as *Big Brother*, staggeringly boring though that would appear to be. For there is a strong possibility that those watching will do just that – watch, rather than listen. Yes, they will note when a councillor says something daft – and most of us have done that (I achieved it with regularity) – but relevantly, and infinitely more likely, observers will note the habits and character traits plus moments of weakness of members. The sloping off early to catch *Midsomer Murders*; the suffering of 'lapses of concentration', accompanied by closed eyes; during debate, facial expressions registering frustration, incredulity, boredom, annoyance, intolerance, impatience – this will be there for all to see, note, and probably disapprove of. To all these failings, and more, I was guilty but shielded by anonymity. With this move into the cyber age, though, that is no longer the case.

Whilst I wish good fortune to those who took this valiant decision I am relieved not to be involved.

43

Dreckly

IT is said that 'procrastination is the thief of time'; also it can be extremely irritating. In many instances failure to activate promised action is cynical, the desire by someone – often the case, some organisation or authority – to avoid implementing agreed policy, or intent, because it is something they do not wish to do, or as is increasingly the case with governments and councils, cannot afford to do.

At other times, mind you, it might well be due to lethargy, lack of will or chronic indecision, the prevarication of people who cannot stir themselves to act or are bereft of the confidence to do so; folk who 'huff and puff' but blow no houses down, who talk and pontificate but fail to 'do' – and are imbued with the sense of urgency of the Trumpton Fire Brigade.

There are some professions who have made this into an art form – the legal one especially; try buying or selling a house. A young relative of ours recently was involved in purchasing his first property; all was, in theory, as simple and straightforward as it was possible to be. The dwelling was empty, he was a cash buyer (thus there was no 'chain'), a price was agreed, necessary funds were in place – yet the transaction took almost three months to complete (unnecessarily stressful ones for a young fellow who had worked hard and planned wisely in order to place his feet upon the 'property ladder'), even though the solicitor said they were 'hurrying matters along'; one suspects this only meant that instead of using second class postage, the occasional first class stamp was being employed which would, no doubt, be reflected in the final bill for 'professional services'. Mind you, being a Devonian, I cannot in honesty say there are not times I do not myself indulge in the soft option of delaying until tomorrow, that which should, and assuredly could, be done here and now. So many of us living in this glorious county succumb to such indulgence that we have created a word for it – 'dreckly'.

Many folk who come west to work or retire confuse this with the word 'directly' (understandably), and when informed something will be done, or somebody will come 'dreckly', can often be assailed by feelings of infuriated bemusement when the breakdown truck doesn't arrive post haste to revive their car broken down in the middle of Dartmoor, or it takes weeks for a builder to produce an estimate for that which needs attention quite urgently. It would be a touch hypocritical for me to criticise such lack of action and initiative, as so often in my life, jobs to be done, phone calls to be made, letters to be written, people to be seen, decisions to be made, are cast into the long, weed infested grass of indolence, though in a sense given a dubious respectability (and an assuaging of conscience) by claiming, half heartedly, that all will be attended to 'dreckly'.

On my part I do make the rather pathetic defence that I own up to such a fault and acknowledge how annoying procrastination can be to others, but not everybody feels such guilt or embarrassment. A gent I know – a central heating engineer – was, when I spoke with him recently, a touch offended that a potential client who had moved to the area from 'up country', took him to task because he had failed to fulfil his promise to service the newcomers' gas boiler before winter. 'I didn't say which winter,' he rasped; I doubt he was joking.

Others, whilst acknowledging that the 'dreckly' mindset can be frustrating (to say the least) to those who do not appreciate its finer points, defend their action – or, more accurately, lack of it – in a far more subtle way; rather than giving explanations or merely ignoring complaints, they make lethargic indolence appear an act of wise, even visionary caution, taking the line 'Fools rush in where angels fear to tread'. In a few instances, this can work but not in the majority – after all, if one has a burst pipe, it needs, desperately, a plumber to 'rush in', not come 'dreckly'; if suffering chronic toothache, relief needs to be immediate, not subject to Devonshire 'manyana'.

When pondering such cases I become aware of the, often, selfish folly that is procrastination – just imagine, for instance, the chaos and carnage if local fire brigades actually did approach emergencies in the Trumpton manner. Thus I resolve to mend my ways; I shall jettison sloth in favour of positive, immediate action – 'dreckly'.

44

The Strange Desire
to be Younger

*T*HERE are those or a 'certain age', mainly male but assuredly not exclusively so, who appear to spend far too large a portion of their lives yearning for the impossible – they wish to be younger. Granted that in this age of remarkable innovation and scientific advance, numerous problems are solved, even, at times, seemingly insurmountable barriers overcome, but the shedding of the years is not amongst them – probably never will be.

Reality dictates that, hopefully, this hurdle will never be jumped; in an already overpopulated world, it is not possible to imagine the extent of the mayhem, misery and privations which would engulf mankind if people were able, at whim, to shed a few decades and thus live virtually forever.

Yet so often the plaintive wail from the lips of many folk, 'If only I was 30 years younger'; when really self-pitying it can rise to 40 – but why? What was so good about life and the world when compared to now; what was this 'Utopia' to which many wish to return; indeed, did it exist at all? In my view it did not – it never has and for certain it never will.

True, we of this older generation are probably less sprightly than we were, often our health a little more uncertain, but quality of life can still be high and stress levels low. Most of us will be retired – or, at least, semi – children long since gone out into the world; our time will largely be our own, with a fair amount of it devoted to leisure and relaxation. Few of us will be classed as being wealthy but probably not many will be impoverished, thankfully (although, sadly, some are despite having lived industrious lives). We will, contrary to that which the poet wrote, 'have time to stop and stare,' or to pursue, at our own pace, that which we wish and desire – within the law, of course – the stresses and demands of life often less than we will have known since early adulthood. Think back 30 years, though, and things were so different – or assuredly they were in the lives of Ann and myself. There was a hefty mortgage to pay (frightfully high interest rates back then), a family to raise and sustain – thus a mountain of food, clothes, shoes and so forth to acquire. There was a house – affordable originally only because it was grievously run down – in need of constant attention; meaning, of course, DIY, a pursuit where my loathing is exceeded only by my incompetence, though fortunately I have a spouse very able. These days. a builder will be paid to do it – back then the most we could afford were the materials, so we had to do it ourselves over a long, fraught period of time. Outside there was a jungle-like garden to tame – fighting, for years, the power of nature's free spirit; often evenings and weekends were spent – partially, at least – ferrying sports loving sons to training, matches, events and the likes whilst the occasional one would be spent at school face to face with a teacher, speaking of one's offspring's progress, or lack of it (usually the former, fortunately).

And daily would come the terror of the letterbox as, so often, envelopes would drop through demanding money. Fortunately I have long been married to a lady brilliant at handling a meagre budget (clearly not Greek) who always managed, somehow, to keep us solvent.

Thus difficult times – though happy, fulfilling years none the less; certainly ones which I would not have missed as a member of a loving, vibrant family – which happily I remain. Would I like to return to them? No; I'll stick with now – and hope that 'now' lasts for many more years yet. I'll remain with the free prescriptions, likewise the bus passes; also the four weekly cheque from the Department of Pensions (it could be more, mind you, but it's still gratefully received even though it's been earned over a lifetime); I'll stick with the multitude of TV channels, the sophistication of modern technology (about which, selfishly, I refuse to learn, but am quite happy to enjoy the benefits it brings via the industry of others); also a bonus, shops and licensed premises 'open all hours', the abundance of cafes and takeaways catering for virtually all tastes, foreign travel, quite cheap (relatively speaking), efficient central heating and air conditioning – and so much more. Mind you, there's no guarantee I'll be around long enough to get maximum benefit from it all, but I comfort myself with the saying that 'Only the Good Die Young.'

45

A Colander List

*T*HERE appears, these days, to be a trend for folk to make statements of aspiration either literal or metaphorical – known as 'bucket lists'. Apparently they comprise a catalogue of attainments, proficiencies, perhaps even conquests of danger, which, presumably, they would like to accomplish before 'kicking' the afore mentioned receptacle.

With many, such stated aims will not proceed beyond fanciful desires which meander about the mind when sitting in an armchair in a warm room of a winter's evening, following a decent meal, a glass of 'Scottish wine' clasped lovingly. Others, though, are serious, spending a goodly portion of their mature years scaling mountains, running marathons, scuba diving, sailing single-handedly around the world in a bath and such like. They are, naturally, to be both admired and respected, but, in my jaundiced view, not emulated. I say this with no sense of pride – though with none of shame either, as we all have the right to live life in our own way as long, of course, as we stay within the law and have regard for others.

The fact is that while adventure and possible danger does not faze me, the expending of energy without financial reward does – and always has. Also, even as a young man, I was never imbued with many major aims or ambitions; these days I have but two (both absurd) – to write a best seller and to witness Plymouth Argyle playing Premier League football. Chances of the first are nil, whilst as to the latter, there is more likelihood of the 'Tooth Fairy' becoming Prime Minister. Neither though, could be entered into a list of intent on my part as both are out of my hands.

So no bucket list for me; the opposite, in fact. For while I have enjoyed my life and derived much fulfilment from it, I have always been cursed with a measure of aimlessness, even negativity – which gets worse. Thus my mind now turns not to what I still wish to do in this world, but rather, towards the opposite – those many activities I have never wished to do, skills I've never acquired, physical pursuits I've always avoided and which will, I'm determined, ever remain alien.

The catalogue of such will not be a slim one; indeed, so great is my apathetic negativity that it would take several editions of this newspaper to get them all in. Here, though, are a few items on my – well, seeing as the vessel will be empty, let's call it a 'colander list'.

Among that which I cannot do, and have no desire to learn, is how to swim. The thought of trundling across mountains of sand dunes, then immersing oneself in freezing sea water fills me with horror; I'm quite content with the occasional hot bath, but that's my limit when it comes to embracing the clear liquid. Also, sitting beside it angling has no allure; being among the world's most impatient, if I didn't catch something in the first five minutes then I would be away home.

Then there is pot holing – chancing life and limb in the bowels of the earth, largely in darkness – and letter boxing on Dartmoor, risking hypothermia and disorientation just to search for a stamp pad hidden under some fog shrouded pile of granite. And golf; now I must admit I enjoy watching it on television, but to actually play it – no thanks.

I've never carried an umbrella and never will – it just clutters up a useful hand; and I've never used a strimmer – a machine about the size of a walking stick that can make more noise than a jet plane but which is no more efficient than a good pair of garden shears.

Then there are cryptic crosswords, so totally incomprehensible to me that I do not understand the answers let alone the questions; Sudoku likewise – neither have I ever attempted and never will; after all, life is confusing enough as it is. Also there are the three most fearsome letters in the English language – DIY. Right from early childhood, where I struggled to even tie up shoelaces (and still do), I knew that the understanding of creativity in the home would never be for me; my attitude has never altered – sight of a paint brush or screw driver can induce utter terror.

Orienteering, sailing, photography, arts and crafts, horseriding, camping, cycling – none of these have I ever pursued (except one or two in a very minimal way) and never will.

On a rare, positive note, I would consider doing a bungee jump – but only if the ropes were attached by somebody with an honours degree in tying knots!

*I would consider doing a bungee jump – but only if
the ropes were attached by somebody with an
honours degree in tying knots!*

46

'Mad Dogs', Englishmen & Marathons

'MAD dogs and Englishmen go out in the mid-day sun'; this was one of the best known lines penned by that famous song writer, author, playwright and raconteur (amongst other things) Sir Noel Coward.

Granted, he was describing those from these shores living abroad in tropical climates administering the far flung British Empire, men and women who would not allow the often stifling heat of noon to deter them from going about their business; duty was put before rest – and, anyway, 'Englishmen detesta siesta'.

Now, it must be conceded that even in midsummer, peak temperatures in these islands are rarely excessive, but even if they are, few of us owing allegiance to the Union flag ever baulk at activity – especially when it comes to leisure beneath a searing sun, or, indeed, in cascading rain. As the saying goes 'The British take their pleasures seriously' – so it is likely goodly numbers will pursue recreation in either stifling heat or foul weather with the same zeal reserved for work (more probably); and so very often these, in theory, periods of rest and relaxation will involve exercise – some of it excessive.

Which brings us to marathons and the like. Now despite being the sort of man who sees the walking to Home Park from the car (at least a quarter of a mile) and the hurling of invective at often inept professional footballers as being a major expending of energy, I am father to sons all of whom appear to consider sitting and relaxing as sinful; in this it could be they take after their mother, a lady rarely daunted by anything – especially tiredness.

Our son, David, is certainly of this ilk, having over recent years, run four Plymouth half marathons (and half of one in this area is, when considering the undulating terrain, probably equal to a full one on the level 'plains' of, say, East Anglia). His most recent confrontation of the fearsome challenge was in April; Ann and I arose early one Sunday morning and got him into the city by 8.30am, whereupon he joined the 5,000 or so other runners.

They set off, amidst major razzamatazz, at 9am – so we went to a strategic nearby spot to watch the multitude pass by, special vigilance being applied to the sighting of a fit looking fellow attired in a grey and yellow running top. We had not long to wait, he passing by, in elegant style, looking fresh, alert and happy, seemingly undaunted that there were still a further 12 miles to run.

Those before him, and some following, looked the part – lean, keen, fit, content and at ease with the challenge confronting them. It was not long, however, before a wider range of competitors (literally, in some cases) began to pass by – ever more slowly and laboured.

Spiderman spun by, along with Batman and Superman

(although in this age of mobiles, it's a mystery as to where he found a phone box in which to change) plus goodly numbers of ladles and gents with tops advocating support for the likes of cancer care, youth clubs, medical research for various problems, sports clubs, harriers and the like. Several ran raising funds for that admirable charity, the British Heart Foundation – though in some instances, by their demeanour, it looked as if any funds they raised would have to be used to render them emergency aid well before the run was over.

Part of the fascination in viewing an event such as this is in simply absorbing the vivid panoply of humanity of both genders passing before one's eyes; the big, small, tall, fat, thin, young, old, happy, sad, comical, ridiculous, professional, dutiful, keen, determined and the inspirational; all were there – and more; some took it very seriously – 'in it to win it', as the television programme states – others there to raise money for their causes, some to confront a challenge, possibly a number because of a dare or a wager; and, no doubt, there were those who felt it was something they wished to achieve just once in their lifetime.

Also, in our nation of rugged eccentrics, probably there were folk of estimable, but assuredly individual character, doing it for fun!

And Dave? He did admirably, coming home in an excellent time well before the bulk of runners. Meeting him afterwards, be produced a bag of 'goodies' presented to all competitors at the finish. From it he brought forth a small packet of biscuits clearly intended to restore energy; he didn't want them so they were put to restoring mine, much needed as I was faced with the challenge of driving 13 miles home – and over hilly terrain.

47

Patience
& the Lack of It

'*P*ATIENCE is a virtue, possess it if you can – rarely found in women, never in a man'; sayings do not come much more sexist than this, a favourite one of an aunt of mine some years ago. The problem is – there is much truth in it.

There are, mind you, some ladies who are very impatient (usually with men) just as there are gents possessing almost saintly amounts – found in sizeable numbers at Home Park waiting for Argyle to score a goal. Generally, though, the female of the species is imbued with greater patience (probably tolerance, also) than the male.

I would have to concede that well to the fore of my own manifold, wide ranging faults is a chronic impatience. When finally I 'pass over' I fear I will become annoyed if St Peter, or more realistically 'Old Nick', is late coming to collect me; shamefully, if there was a 'Richter Scale' measuring such a fault, I would register the full 10.

In a restaurant, even though I enjoy good food, I would sooner have egg and chips if it took but five minutes to prepare, than a sublime creation by Michel Roux if it took 45. If caught in traffic, I find the first exit road possible, then meander all around the houses (literally) and lanes to arrive at my planned destination probably later than if I had stayed with it; daft, of course, but then that's the nature of the beast.

I will have used more time, energy and fuel, and engendered more stress, than if I had simply settled down and remained in the line of vehicles. Logic, though, comes not into such matters. Perhaps folk such as myself – and we are not few in number – should muse upon the words of poet W. H. Davies – '*What is this life if full of care, we have no time to stand and stare?*'

There is, mind you, another side to this, that which provokes impatience; that which can make it understand-able. A visit, say, to the dentist – a precise time stated for the appointment; the patient arrives in ample time but some half hour later is still sitting in the waiting room reading a five-year-old 'Reader's Digest'; even the, generally, slight discomfort endured in the chair and the very real pain when having to pay, register less, surely, than the wasting of a busy person's time. And then there are shops; there is a fairly priced, well stocked popular local store, staffed by charming, helpful, diligent ladies and gentlemen; the problem, though, is that dearly there are too few of them. Whenever it gets busy, queues form at the tills, often snaking away towards the horizon; a message will then go out over the tannoy – 'Colleague announcement; queue busters to the checkouts please.' I overheard one day from a fellow who had over the years spent many an hour in the slow moving line (and was a touch worried that the bread he was carrying would be stale before he got to pay for it) – 'there's more chance of seeing the SAS.'

Now I'm told that these 'queue busters' exist because they have been seen, but as even the great David Attenborough has not been able, it would seem, to have them captured on film, they must be rare to the point of being almost extinct; sadly, so many supermarkets seem to be understaffed.

There are a few shopkeepers also who do not provide the greatest service to potential customers. At times official opening periods are displayed which seem works of fiction. The owners appearing to open and close at their convenience rather than that of their potential clients. Many traders – plus the chamber of commerce – often comment as to how crucial is the vitality of small, town centre shops; quite right, but they need to be open!

None of this, though, can fire me to the level of fury I felt a few years ago when visiting an excellent local entertainment facility to see a well known, popular folk group. They were due on stage at 7.30pm, but there was no sign of them at 8pm. Irate, I went to enquire what the problem was and was told, in casual, unapologetic tones, 'Oh, they never start on time.' Had it not been I'd paid several 'bob' to see them, I'd have gone home there and then; I have never, however, booked to see them again, good though they are. Mind you, they're welcome to come and see me; it will cost them nothing, but they had better be on time!

48

Sayings

M Y mother could quote more sayings and adages than you could 'shake a stick at'. Being a countrywoman from a farming family living for generations in the Tamar Valley, and herself earning a 'crust' from the land, many concerned that which dominates, inevitably, the minds of folk who are ever hostages to its vagaries – the weather.

Many of her pronouncements, ever the way with those in such occupations, were of a pessimistic nature. She would never be fooled by a bright, promising early morning in summer; no, for usually she would opine, 'Sun before seven, rain before 11,' or simply, 'Too bright, too early.' Sadly, all too often she was right, positive initial prospects rapidly giving way to precipitation. It never distressed her, though, for no matter how adverse the elements, she would state, with confidence, that there would always be 'seed time and harvest' – quite correctly, of course. Her climatic predictions also came more long term; a cold, late autumn would invoke, regularly, her comment, 'Ice in November which will bear a duck, rest of the winter mire and muck'; often there was truth in this, as an unseasonably cold pre-Yuletide frequently would be the harbinger of a mild winter. Mind you, she also had the opposite covered, for if the weeks up to, and including the festive season were relatively balmy, from her would come, 'A green Christmas fills the churchyard'; dramatic words clearly, and alarming to grave diggers, but once again not without foundation as most of the severe winters of the past century or so were preceded by weeks of higher than average temperatures.

Sooth-saying regarding summer would also come from her lips, as she, like many others, would note in early springtime the race between oak and ash to refoliate for the long days. Here, though, she could get somewhat confused, as she would mouth predictions which contradicted each other. Often she would state 'oak before ash, we'll only get a splash – ash before oak we're sure to get a soak'; another time, though – perhaps even in the same week – she would say, chirpily, 'Oak before ash we're sure to get a soak, ash before oak, we'll only have a croak'; a strange word 'croak' having no definition beyond the sounds emitted by frogs (according to dictionaries) but in mother's mind it meant a shortage of rain; possibly it was a good Devonshire dialect term. The 'pearls' which fell from her lips, however, covered much more than the weather. If one of her sons complained about something concerning that to which there was no obvious solution, she would state simply, 'What can't be cured must be endured'; if someone articulated pity in an adverse situation, but offered no remedy, then she would give the view – 'Sympathy without relief is like mustard without beef.'

Sayings

A lady of mature age who attired herself in raiment more suited to somebody of lesser years, would be termed, 'an old yaw dressed up lamb fashion'; somebody, of either gender, who was a touch downtrodden or put upon, as being like a 'toad under a harve' (Devonshire for a harrow), whilst somebody who could not be entrusted confidently with a task, would evoke the more basic comment – 'about as reliable as a cheel's behind' (a cheel being local dialect for a small child).

Those who filled a plate with a large portion of food but then failed to eat it would have 'eyes bigger than their belly', whilst someone in life, a touch out of their depth in some matter, if not assisted, would 'Perish like a robin on a branch'; a strange one, this, as robins appear to be very resilient birds.

Many of these adages were widely used – some possibly still are; there were a few, though, which I recall only being uttered by mother. The strangest of these – possibly incomprehensible – were the words in coming across a situation, or a venue, where chaos reigned; 'It's like a dance in jail,' she would say. With hindsight I should have asked her where such a saying came from; sadly it is much too late now. Not that it is unique in being obscure; there are many others and possibly none more bizarre – perhaps even daft – than the one invoked when the apprentice attempts to instruct the experienced – 'Don't teach your grandmother how to suck eggs.' What does it mean? How many grannies have done this – and why would they? Daft? Possibly – yet like all such adages, including those of mother, they enrich our glorious language and should be kept alive.

49

Phrases & Slogans

*I*T had not been the best of Saturdays; Argyle had lost, the postman had delivered a fistful of bills, the rain and wind had not ceased. It got no better, for half way through the evening I remembered the car was low on petrol, so, as we were away on a longish journey very early next morning, the tank needed filling right away.

Thus at 9.30pm did I replenish supplies, then proffer a credit card in payment. Having a 'senior moment', I could not recall the relevant pin number so paid with a debit instead – a beleaguered bank account being further 'mugged', instantly. By this time my will to live was weak, getting ever more feeble – then almost destroyed by the lady at the till. Smiling pleasantly, she returned my card, then uttered four words which were as inappropriate, pointless, even plain daft, as any I'd heard in many a day – 'Have a nice day.'

I opened my mouth to point out that there were only about two hours remaining, the previous 22 had been a pain and all I looked forward to was midnight when it would be over – but had not the energy. Rather, I smiled bleakly, thanked her, and went on my way.

There have been many fatuous affectations which have afflicted us from the USA, but few, surely, more annoying than this. Then there is 'bon appetit' – though the 'Yanks' can't be blamed for this. When it is spoken to a diner in a French restaurant by a Gallic waiter, fair enough, but the last time it was said to me was when receiving a ploughman's lunch in a 'spit and sawdust' pub (come to think of it, not much sawdust) from the landlord – in a Geordie accent. To be fair, some establishments do use English when mouthing platitudes to diners, the word 'enjoy' often coming from the lips of waiting staff; the problem though is that, at times, such is spoken with all the bonhomie of a rottweiler, in tones of curt instruction rather than gentle goodwill.

Unfortunately modern life is littered with such routine phrases and exhortations spoken mindlessly and auto- matically. A solid example of this recently was when I made purchases in a local supermarket. The young gent at the checkout greeted me courteously then launched into his standard query: 'Would you like help with your packing?' I thanked him, but suggested that as all I had was a packet of polo mints and a daily paper, even a doddery old fool like me could cope – just. It is, mind you, probably a touch unfair to find fault with this – after all, basic good manners and thought for others are involved and should always be welcomed, indeed applauded; it would be so much more effective though and appreciated, if consideration was given to the appropriateness of the words before being spoken.

What jar more, however (well, they certainly do me) are slogans, usually written – especially in advertisements –

h

which are at best banal, at worse irritatingly absurd. One which comes to mind is 'Large enough to cope, small enough to care.' Builders often use this jingle when touting for work and, in principle, there is nothing amiss when used by a firm of modest size which well might deliver on the promise. The trouble is, though, it can appear in the script of a 'one man band', who might well care but clearly can only cope with very small jobs; also at times, in the screed of a company geared up to build an entire estate; they can probably cope, and may well care, but small?

Then there is the use of the word 'passionate', employed confetti-like, to try to convince the potential customer of the dedicated zeal of the possible supplier; eating houses are 'passionate about food,' clothes shops likewise about fashion, and so forth. There is nothing wrong with exhortations to use a company's services, or purchase a shop's wares – but please let us have a touch of originality. This, though, is minor compared to standard phrases employed by 'helplines', set up by the likes of banks, the utilities and national companies; these surely are the ones which really infuriate. Firstly come options, the complexity of which would tax the deductive powers of Sherlock Holmes; if fortunate enough to locate the correct one a disembodied voice informs 'This call may be recorded for training purposes'. Mind you, no need to fret over invasion of privacy as chances of talking to a live person are remote. Discordant music will come down the line, interspersed with the request 'Please hold – your call is important to us.' Really? If that is so, why not employ sufficient staff to ensure it is answered before despair – or worse, murderous intent – takes over.

50

A Cornish Holiday Let

*T*o commence with positives. The weather was fair, the food splendid, the wine flowed like the Tavy in spate, the company delightful.

A family holiday (a goodly number of our scattered 'tribe', anyway), down in the Duchy. Matt and Avisa, with three of our grandchildren, jetted into Heathrow from Hong Kong; another granddaughter, Jasmine, joined us from London, along with Avisa's parents, Masoud and Soudi, plus Matt's twin brother Dave who had crossed the Tamar from Brentor.

A 'four star' holiday home had been hired – and anticipation was high amongst all. Living nearest, Ann and I were the first to arrive in the house on a hill near Wadebridge. We were due to take occupancy at 3pm and, to the minute, we were there. We were not alone; a lady appeared mop in hand, a startled expression upon her face, 'Oh, you're here already!' We pointed out it was the appropriate hour as stated in the brochure, to which she rejoined: 'Oh yes – well, I've almost finished the cleaning.' This turned out to be an exaggeration, as an hour later she was still beavering away with the hoover.

We took the sole course open to proud Britons – made tea, then went outside to leave the good lady in peace, expecting to enjoy a refreshing cup of Earl Grey, relaxing in the sun. Now, the beverage was up to standard but the resting side was not. There was a gent trundling up and down the lawn cutting, noisily, the verdant pasture; clearly his remit did not include work on flower beds, some of which sported weeds the size of triffids. He was not alone for also there was a fellow hosing the outside of the windows.

Eventually, all was done, and peace, inside and out, reigned – too much of it. For we had a call from the London contingent; they would be delayed for a couple of hours due to traffic problems. Eventually though, they arrived; an enjoyable week together was both expected and realised – despite the deficiencies of our temporary home.

Whilst the building itself was a well built Victorian former farmhouse, the internal layout appeared to have been designed by a fitness instructor for the SAS; certainly relaxation was not to be tolerated. The dining room was a considerable distance from the kitchen, heading north, but the crockery and glasses were in cupboards towards the east. With 11 to cater for, a rota system of native bearers (mainly grandchildren) was compiled, they transporting whatever was required.

The cooking itself was superb (amongst my many good fortunes is to be married, father and father-in-law, to accomplished chefs), despite a dearth of essential utensils, plus rust in others and a cooker more temperamental than an Italian prima donna. After a meal, the washing-up; nothing to worry about here, as there was a dishwasher. But where?

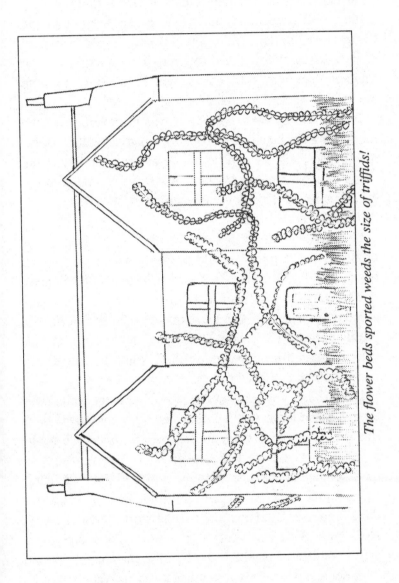

The flower beds sported weeds the size of triffids!

After a long, exhaustive search, it was located in a far distant utility room to the west, so far away that the bearers (rota system still applying) needed a refreshment stop halfway. Even then, though, it was closer to the kitchen than was the freezer which, possibly to save electricity, seemed to be halfway to the Arctic.

It gets worse; next morning it was discovered that the main thing the machine did not do was to actually cleanse the dishes. Thus, once more, a long distance hauling of the chinaware back to the kitchen sink to be scrubbed in the traditional way. This done – eventually (there was a lot of it) time for breakfast.

On went the toaster and, after an age, up it popped; the problem was, a tourist would probably gain a greater tan from a holiday, in winter, in the Orkneys than did the bread.

The Dunkirk spirit kicked in – let's get out of the house and have a barbecue; there was one on the patio. A further problem, though – it would not ignite, and even if it had, it was lathered in more grease than would be found in a dozen fish and chip shops.

Despite all, we enjoyed our days and slept well, even though the mattresses felt like paving slabs covered in linen. There were two avenues, however, where we could have no worries; we were never likely to oversleep, as ours seemed to be one of only two buildings in many square miles of countryside; the other, an industrial workshop, was sited next door – and work started, noisily, at 6:30am. Also our safety was assured; for there was a sign emblazoned on the wall – 'In the case of fire, phone 999; nearest phone box two miles away in Wadebridge.'

Overall verdict. Family, five stars – house, 'interesting'.

51

The Suffering of 'Fools'

*T*HERE are some folk who admire in others character traits with which, personally, I am uneasy. The diversity of human nature means, inevitably, that which is seen by some as a positive quality in a person, to others is a fault.

One which comes to mind – well, to mine at least – is the observation uttered by some in rather admiring tones when assessing a man's character (and it is usually someone of the male gender), 'he does not (or did not if deceased) suffer fools gladly.' It has never been a judgement with which I have sympathy; assuredly, if someone said such of me after 'I had shuffled off this mortal coil', I would not see it as a compliment.

Probably it is helpful here to quote the dictionary definition of the word 'fool'; the Oxford states, 'simpleton, dupe, silly person.' Now possibly there are those who assess the IQ of others in such a disparaging and rather cruel way; it could on rare occasions be technically correct though callous and unnecessary; but it is not unfair to suspect that many class as 'idiots' those with whom they disagree – or who retain radically different opinions, outlooks and convictions. Someone whose political views are well to the right might use the word 'fool', in contempt, when commenting on the ideals of a person of the left – and vice versa, of course. In either direction, such folk are not daft – merely, they are possessing of different beliefs, possibly living by dissimilar principles; they should not be vilified – on the contrary, their views of life and the world should at least be tolerated, hopefully respected. Those who 'do not suffer fools' could be charged with not only lacking in regard for the independent lifestyle and thoughts of others, but worse, to be bigoted – not, surely, an attitude to be admired or praised; after all, one person's 'fool' can be another's genius.

Another cry which comes from the lips of good citizens (often northerners it must be said but by no means exclusively) – 'I say it as I see it', or even more bluntly 'I call a spade, a spade.' Many will state such with pride, seemingly convinced that frankness – rudeness, all too often – is a virtue, that their right to express personal opinions and judgements supercedes those of others; that they are justified in expressing views even though these might be hurtful, even offensive to many. Again such have supporters – 'He's a real Joe Blunt,' or 'He takes no prisoners,' and the like, will be spoken admiringly by those sympathetic to them or their apologists; this, plus the passive acceptance of unyielding self opinion, sometimes outright bigotry, is surely misguided. For essentially here we are talking of prejudice, intolerance, self-righteousness, blinkered outlooks, often ill-informed convictions; there is little here to respect, and nothing to admire.

Acceptance of the rights of people to live as they desire – as long as they keep within the law and have regard for the way of life of those around them – is essential to the cohesion of a civilised society; tolerance of others, no matter how different their lifestyle, beliefs, principles, whims – all these have long been to the fore in our great country and, overall, remain so. Is this not the reason why so many of other lands, religions, origins, creeds desire to come here to live? Not that we do not at times feel prejudice and bias; we should not experience guilt if we do, for it is a natural human reaction and emotion; even Jesus succumbed – did he not eject money lenders from the synagogue even though they were breaking no laws? Indeed there would be few people in this world who feel no bias against somebody – and probably fewer groups who suffer none.

Asylum seekers, economic migrants (and there is a difference between the two), gays, ethnic minorities, smokers, followers of various religions, believers in none, the disabled, blind, deaf, the fat, thin, short, tall; those who are left-handed, the exceedingly clever, folk with learning difficulties, those who talk a lot, or very little, perhaps who stutter – the list of citizenry who will encounter prejudice is manifold, indeed, little short of endless; as, mind you, is that of those who exhibit such hostility towards the ways, dogmas, habits and idiosyncracies of others.

Yet nobody has the right to belittle, mock, abuse – at times, frankly, persecute those whose ways offend them. Still, fortunately those who sail through life on seas of intolerance are probably outnumbered by the folk who readily 'suffer fools gladly'.

Having said this, if honest I would have to admit to the occasional bias regarding colour – I feel illogical enmity towards any football fan whose favourite shirt's shade is not that of a special, rich green with a 'Mayflower' motif printed upon it.

52

Yellow – Plusses & Minuses

DAWDLING in the street talking about football, the state of the nation, weather, television and other crucial topics, suddenly was I galvanised into urgent action; thus did I stagger along the pavement in an attempt – vain – to avert calamity, albeit, a minor one.

For there at the far end of it I had espied a fellow clearly on official business – not difficult, despite the distance, as he wore a florescent yellow jacket. He appeared to be writing – indeed, I knew he was, and was aware of the use to which he was putting his pen; assuredly he was not scribbling his shopping list. Despite my haste, when I reached the danger zone he had gone, so I was unable to plead my case, offer excuses and beg for mercy. Not that it would have done any good; after all, the gent was only doing his job, something of which I was well aware as I pulled the cellophane covered parking ticket from the windscreen.

Even if I'd confronted him, I could not have argued a case – I was guilty as a fox in a henhouse; indeed, if I had left the car parked there much longer it is possible a zealous conservation official might have listed it as an item of historical significance.

After paying my fine, it occurred to me just how large a role, in public places, is played by people donning, predominantly, vivid yellow – and how varied are our reactions to them. Viewed in a positive light are the gents (and they seem overwhelmingly male) who empty the bins. A hardworking group, in weather fair – but all too often foul – they can be seen hurtling through the streets in the same vibrant colours as Usain Bolt; granted, not quite as fast, but one wonders just how swift would be the Jamaican if laden with a full recycling box; only the most impatient of motorists will ever honk a horn if delayed briefly and usually it is just that.

Then there are the emergency services; sight of police, firefighters and paramedics ministering – urgently – to folk trapped roadside, in a wreck of a car, is never less than concerning. However, to see the canary hued rescue personnel rendering aid, reassures; for those in distress – possibly, mortal danger – are being helped by professionals; it could be their lives are being saved.

Very different, though, is one's reaction when, upon the highway, another police car, ablaze with flashing lights, looms in the rear mirror, approaching, seemingly, with the speed of a bullet. One is engulfed with angst – perhaps even mild terror; the speedometer takes priority, thus often the foot brake is applied – sometimes severely – then, usually, relief as the siren wailing vehicle rockets past. Clearly, someone, somewhere, is in trouble, possibly their own fault, but perhaps not; whatever, self preservation dominates – 'It's nothing to do with me' – so pressure upon the accelerator will increase once more; not right, true, but on occasions impatience rules.

Often, mind you, the sight of folk in daffodil colours merely annoys; roadworks are to the fore in this direction. To a degree, hypocrisy features at such times; for so many of us grumble about the chronic state of road surfaces, the need for upgrading a highway, perhaps just the need for hedge trimming on a narrow lane. Yet when the contractors actually tackle such, we are upset because the way ahead is impeded by traffic lights – workers in, crucially, easily visible yellow, often huge vehicles ripping up old, or laying new surfaces, having priority.

An illogical matter, of course, and an unfair one. After all, there is no great prospect of such vital work being done by fairies in the middle of the night. Likewise when those working for the utilities – gas, water, electricity and so forth – decide to erect barriers. For certain they are not digging in search of oil, rather to repair or renew ancient pipes, mains and the like – but it can still incur the wrath of motorists when sat in a queue of traffic, engine idling, temporary lights seemingly stuck on red.

Thus are we, when on the Queen's Highway, so often in the hands of those garbed in daffodil colours. It can, naturally, be irksome, at times infuriating, yet all these official workers fulfil a purpose – even the traffic warden, or, to give them their modern name, 'Civil Enforcement Officer (parking)'; without them, congestion would reign supreme. Having said this, that gentleman, that day, cost me £30. It still wrankles even though it served me right – and I've not done it since (or perhaps to be more honest, luckily I've not been caught!).

181

53

A Holiday North of the Border

*A*nn saw it in the pages of this treasured local newspaper, a large advertisement of interest to us both, though I, about as observant as the average mole, had failed to notice it. Five days in Scotland in October (thus post midges) was promised; flying from Exeter to Edinburgh, then a coach journey to a hotel south of Inverness.

There would follow a few days of organised rail and coach travel across the north of that sparsely populated land. Now whilst Ann had been north of the border for a holiday – though a very long time ago – I never have. Thanks to the great generosity of my family I once trod the awesomely bleak, lonely terrain of Tibet and stood in the foothills of Mount Everest but never had I been within 400 miles of the Highlands of Scotland. Before that Loch Ness pair, Salmond and Sturgeon, closed the borders, it was time to put such matters right – time to venture north.

Flying in from different parts of England, the group met up at the airport of Scotland's capital; a comfortable coach awaited as did, it transpired, a most competent, cheerful driver and a first class courier – a gentleman of charm, knowledge and patience who gave the impression of actually enjoying his work.

The tour party – some 40 in number – were, inevitably, a motley collection of humanity; the long, short and tall, the thin, large, extra large; the gentle, noisy, dour, ebullient; the optimist and the reverse. There was something, though, most of us had in common – we were of a 'certain age'. Indeed, we could have doubled as extras for *Last of the Summer Wine* – more sticks to be seen than in a hockey match.

The itinerary was mind concentrating – assuredly not suited to anyone seeking leisurely relaxation. Up before dawn, the first stop was the dining room where was consumed – by me, at least – a gargantuan 'full Scottish' breakfast (uncannily identical to the 'full English'). At home a scrap of toast and a bowl of cereal usually suffice, but with this early meal included in the package, the quest for value for money made it crucial.

Sufficient calories were absorbed to last till evening, when dinner – also part of the deal – would be devoured; lunchtimes, thus, needed little more than the buying of beverages. Before 9am we would be on the move, taking to the mainly single lane roads; the plus, however, as this domain is lightly peopled – even by Devon and Cornwall standards – was that traffic between the few towns was modest, schedules, therefore, easy to maintain. Our road travel was interspersed, daily, with rail journeys through glorious terrain where one could absorb the grandeur, solitude and singularity of the Highlands.

These excursions included a journey up a mountain in the Cairngorms courtesy of a funicular railway. At its base it was nippy, at the summit six inches of snow and a bitter wind; the views, though, were magnificent – and there was some decent mulled wine, also.

Late afternoon we would be delivered back to our hotel with probably insufficient energy amongst us to power a 40 watt light bulb; there was, though, sufficient resilience within us to confront the excellent dinners provided, but widespread deafness abounded when invited to join in the evening entertainment in the hotel – a boisterous ceilidh; traditional, true, but few of our party were up for it – though Ann with her lightness of foot and sense of rhythm might well have been. Sadly she had no partner, her husband having the dancing ability of a duckbilled platypus. Mind you, the music, though clearly Celtic, was not needed in terms of making us aware we were in Scotland – a very different part of the United Kingdom. The 'Saltire' flies from 90 per cent of flagpoles, the Union Flag rarely seen; book and gift shops overflow with tales of Scottish history, mementoes shrouded in tartan, local delights taken by mouth – whisky and shortbread in abundance (major plusses) – and, in one large shop, a multitude of mugs.

From a distance they looked quite attractive but on closer inspection, they celebrated the Battle of Bannockburn, the most famous of the few victories of the Scots over the 'Sassenachs'. With most visitors coming from south of Hadrian's Wall, they were clearly a slow seller. Still, although nationalism would appear to be sweeping across this northern land like a tsunami, folk on the whole were welcoming and friendly; certainly they had no aversion to English banknotes.

So, an enjoyable holiday – a touch nonplussing for a 'grumpy old man' who likes to moan; we must try Wales next year – that might return matters back to normal (though I have to be careful in this direction as my wife is half Welsh)!

54

Wembley

W
e're on our way to Wembley, we shall not be moved';
a famous chant this, and one to be treasured; for when
one considers the multitude of football clubs of varying
levels and accomplishments scattered about this land,
relatively few actually get to tread the hallowed turf.

Whilst Plymouth Argyle did appear at the old Wembley
(originally entitled 'the Empire Stadium') 20 years ago,
this Spring Bank Holiday Monday was the first time they
had earned the right to do battle on the emerald surface of
the new. Back in 1996 they were there to contest the
second division play-off final (versus Darlington that
time), and it was a similar situation last month, the golden
reward for victory, promotion to division one – the
opponents, AFC Wimbledon.

However, whilst the first part of the chant (articulating
the North London location) was accurate, the second
assuredly was not, for a mammoth amount of movement
was involved; to go from Devon – many also, from south
of the Tamar – required a vast amount of transportation, up
to 300 miles of it in fact, probably more for some.

Now, support for the Pilgrims has ever been mercurial; when performances and, even more importantly, results, are very bad, then the Green Army, at times seemingly struggle to outnumber those commanded by Captain Mainwaring at Walmington-on-Sea. When matters take a major turn for the better, however, and even more alluring, this legendary ground is allotted to be the cauldron for vital football action, then the ranks of the South West army become like 'Topsy' – they just grow and grow; in consequence a multitude gathered to sally forth in support of this long established (1886), famous old club, the most southernly professional outfit in Britain.

Thus it was on that fateful Monday morning, a mighty Armada set off from around the far South West heading for London – though by motorway rather than by sea. All lanes of the M5 and M4 heading north were thronged by vehicles of radical diversity in size, shape, age, quality, and probably, safety. On the outside track, mainly cars driven by those anxious to savour the awaiting atmosphere as soon as possible; in the middle, vehicles of varying descriptions including many coaches; on the inside truly a motley selection of transport, some, especially buses, of a vintage going back the best part of half a century. No doubt they had been MOT tested – but possibly not for some years.

Being on the nearest lane was for them an act of wisdom as they could go slowly – and there was, crucially, the hard shoulder, a surface upon which many were parked, prematurely; one suspects that, sadly, not all would have made London. And on this long foray to the capital there was colour -- or, one to be exact – green; flags, scarves, streamers all flowing and fluttering from the cavalcade sweeping ever closer (well most of them, at least) to the 90,000 seater auditorium where, it was hoped, an end would be brought to what has been for the Plymouth club – and supporters – a decade of failure and despair.

A few years back, the Pilgrims suffered consecutive relegations from the Championship down to Division Two; worse, they almost slid into oblivion, decimated by debt. Thus victory – and promotion – via triumph at Wembley, would be as sweet as honey. Despite the show of exuberance and optimism from many, there were amongst this mighty, irresistible, ebullient 'green horde' (assuredly less malevolent than Genghis Khan's golden one) a goodly number of supporters (certainly the regulars) more than a touch nervous and apprehensive; to them this was more than a potentially exciting adventure – it was a crusade.

Eventually, following a painfully slow, almost stressful meandering across the leviathan that is London, the national stadium was reached. It is a sight to make one stand and stare, an awesome 21st century colosseum of enormity, yet possessing of both style and grace; certainly a majestic, atmospheric amphitheatre to view the clash of modern day gladiators – armed with studded boots, attired (in this instance) on the one side in blue, the other in the 'sacred' green. However, whilst colours on the pitch were evenly matched the situation in the stadium was very different; 60,000, or so, was the attendance – but two thirds of the fans sported the emerald shade; assuredly they made the most noise. Did it have the desired effect? Sadly, no!

Unlike the Roman army of Caesar, whilst the Green one 'came' and 'saw' – they did not 'conquer'. That was because the 'Dons', on the day, were selfish and refused to allow the Pilgrim legions a joyful return home; rather, they had the temerity to win. Oh well, there's always next season – which will be upon us far too soon.

55

Shopping

*I*N an era when there seems to be three year courses to cover everything from water divining to tarot card reading, from bird watching to surfing, it is possibly surprising there are not degrees (honours) in shopping.

Here, a personal admission – I would fail lamentably; only in technical matters could I be more inept, obtuse and, frankly, disinterested. If it cannot be consumed by mouth then I can see little point in it being purchased; granted this is a dinosaur like mentality with 'luddite' tendencies – a fact pointed out to me by my family. If the human race had progressed at a pace dictated by reactionaries like me, then we would still be cave dwellers and 'hunter gatherers' – and I fear I would not be any good at that either.

The longer I live, however, the more I appreciate that successful, safe and relatively stress free navigation of the turbulent ocean that is retail, requires a subtle mix of education, vision, wisdom and discipline; it is an art and a science, so those mastering it (amazingly, to me, some do) should be awarded, surely, degrees in both from the nation's prestigious seats of learning. My wife, Ann, is rare in that whilst she is a master of the arcane challenge that is shopping, she does not enjoy it, looking upon it as that which has to be confronted, rather than 'therapy'.

From time to time, though, it is a case of 'When needs must' – and the fact that, nobly, she is willing to buy for me as well is, in my direction, joyously received. There is the odd occasion I cannot escape, such as when shoes need to be tried on or my opinion is required in the selection of gifts for family, but much in the area of clothes she purchases in my absence, aware of my size, my conservative tastes – and that I appear to have the blood of a lizard, often feeling cold in a heatwave.

Then there are supermarkets – the gathering of victuals and liquor to sustain life. Ann compiles the list and naturally (also mercifully) makes the decisions, but often I go along with her to help with the numerous heavy bags. Still, physically demanding though forays to shops, department stores and supermarkets are, success relies on the use of the 'little grey cells' in often Machiavellian like preparation which can tax the sharpest mind and which warrants recognition from the higher echelons of academia.

Firstly, especially with food halls, comes the compilation of 'the list'; in itself, this is not complicated – filling the trolley is. Getting best value, negotiating the 'chicanes' known as aisles, neutralising the irritation of empty shelves with 'special offers' printed above, trying to calculate relative costs when items are labelled in obscure metric weights rarely divisible by ten (which, surely, should be metrication's principal attribute); attempting to locate sell-by dates, finding items not bought on a regular basis (often, attempting to access those which are); ensuring there is sufficient expenditure to activate the '£5 off' voucher (but not greatly in excess, as such would reduce any major gain) – this, and more, is the assault course termed 'the weekly shop'.

There then remains the fraught challenge of the checkouts; at busy times getting through them unscathed can instil a touch of euphoria; possibly such deserving of a chapter to itself. This, however, stressful though it may be, is relatively simple compared to acquiring non-food items in stores and shops. Initially there are the vital decisions concerning what actually to buy; after all, there's nothing complex in choosing a tin of beans, but multiple considerations come into focus when purchasing, say, clothes, whether female or male. Colour, style, fashion, size, suitability, price; these factors and more come into play – truly a laborious, stressful exercise.

This is not the end of the matter, though, for those decisions having been made, there follows the intellectually challenging process of paying. Ten per cent discount on one item, perhaps twenty on another, but only if one possesses the relevant store card, or if it's not in a sale, or there is an 'R' in the month. Vouchers possibly to be redeemed, but only on limited goods and only if it is a leap year.

Thus a traumatic, highly disciplined business which seemingly can only be executed with real success by someone with shrewd judgement, strong character, an intellect of Mensa proportions, the heart of a lion and the patience of a saint. . . and the 'flexible' friendship of a credit card (or plural) also helps – immensely.

Ensuring there is sufficient expenditure to activate the '£5 off' voucher!

j

56

Political Parties

*I*N quiet moments, it can be a diversion to consider the origins of various aspects of life today – its institutions, customs, beliefs and so forth. For instance those interested in current affairs and the way the world is run and governed might muse as to the derivation of political movements and parties.

In this direction, folk will see matters very differently (though there could possibly be consensus on some). For instance, it could be argued that the first communist was not Karl Marx; granted he articulated the theory but did not really live by its creed; however, a man who did, almost 2,000 years ago was Jesus of Nazareth. Always he preached tolerance and mutual respect; men and women should not covet that of others, should eschew war and antagonism – indeed, should dwell together in harmony and love. This, in a sense, is communism – or certainly that philosophy at its best, the sharing of the world's goodwill and bounty thanks largely to the nobility of the human spirit.

The problem, though, is that Christ, not being mortal in

the true sense, did not understand the frailties, avarice, ambitions and desires of those about him; sadly human nature will usually trump the principled integrity of pure communism. Socialism, however, has a more worldly base; yet it remains difficult to make it work effectively. One jaundiced cynic, when asked as to whom he thought was the first true socialist, suggested it was Christopher Columbus, in that when undertaking his epic journey to the Americas, 'he started out not knowing where he was going, when he got there he didn't know where he was, he arrived back home not knowing where he had been – and did the entire trip on borrowed money.'

As to the first 'Green', a strong case could be made for Genghis Khan. Now, this might seem a strange choice; after all, he was a brutal man who led a terrifying army that created the largest empire the world has ever known, butchering vast numbers of hapless folk in the process. Yet he did it in a way which, even by the standards of our times, was laudably environmentally friendly. For his fearsome troops carried all they needed on their horses – no wagon trains or caravans; he built no cities, manufactured no goods, created no agriculture or infrastructure; he and his 'Golden Horde' just lived off the land about them as they passed through, pillaging at will. So, no carbon emissions here (except possibly from the horses), no building on flood plains – no real pollution at all; mind you, life would have been a touch difficult if one had been a vegetarian – even worse, vegan.

Several can spring to mind when ascertaining the first Conservative; a strong case though could be made for Henry VIII; here was a man quite shrewd on the financial front, a builder of strong defence forces and reasonably popular with the people. Yet his personal life was riven with marital strife and infidelity not totally dissimilar to some prominent members of the Tory party over the years; he was fortunate there was no press around at the time to expose such (though even if there had been, it is doubtful they would have dared).

The original Liberal Democrat could well have been Edward the Confessor, a good, even saintly man who seemed cursed with indecision, usually tending to see good in all and both sides of a situation – even potential national calamities – coming down on neither. Thus when England was being terrorised by Vikings he appeared to seek the guidance of the Lord, rather than involving that of his generals. The same is not true of a predecessor – King Alfred; for he, it could be said, was the founder of UKIP. Granted, the United Kingdom was not around when he reigned in the 9th century – nor England, for that matter. These islands then comprised several disparate – perhaps even desperate – states, often warring with each other, thus leaving the land exposed to predatory, marauding Norsemen. Alfred, though, as King of Wessex, managed to engender some unity amongst the kingdoms, and the invaders were largely repelled, though not fully evicted from these islands.

With this, plus the creation of a code of laws, his building of naval ships and his repudiation of Latin in favour of Saxon English as the official language, he laid the foundations for the unified England which came into being not long after his death.

As to the Scottish Nationalist Party, was not Robbie

Burns its creator – albeit inadvertently? Their national poet, his verse is so incomprehensible to many south of the border, it is bound to strengthen the solidarity of those north – though one suspects many of them do not understand it either.

57

The Referendum

*A*S a young man I was advised that while there were a multitude of subjects which could be discussed in public with one giving freely of opinion – even the radical – it was advisable not to extend such boldness of speech to party politics (religion also, to an extent, although there is often much to admire in folk who stand up for their convictions or faith, especially when they risk persecution for doing so – sadly ever present in the world both past and present).

My father, a local councillor for decades (always standing as an Independent) and a man of strong political conviction, always adhered to such discipline. Never would he disclose to others outside of his family his views regarding the machinations of those who shaped our lives at Westminster, often their actions and decisions guided by dogma rather than common sense or the pursuance of fair play.

He was never afraid to speak up on local issues, mind you, but in this arena, in his era (he died in 1971), councillors were almost universally independent. Yet, despite his reticence regarding articulating his views on national issues which might have displayed his political leanings, I feel he would have spoken freely and in partisan fashion in open debate during the recent EU referendum campaign and I suspect I can guess his sympathies.

The reason he would not have felt constrained? Simply the fact that this was not a party political issue – though all the main groupings in Westminster, Wales, Scotland and Northern Ireland tried to make it so, all laying down official party policy and entreating their supports and sympathisers to follow it.

However, a most satisfying aspect of the four months of discussion concerning our future regarding the European Union (in or out) was that official ideological hierarchies exercised little influence. Right wing capitalists and left wing socialists could well be of like mind, while members of local committees of leading political groups were often in dispute – possibly as it should be.

For the momentous decision which the British people were being asked to make had nothing to do, in the direct sense, with the Conservative, Labour, Liberal Democrat, Green, Nationalist or Independence parties, though they clearly had a right to have policies and views.

No, this was a matter for the citizens of this nation, a plebiscite in which every man and woman over the age of 18 had the right to a direct say as to the path we should take; this is the strength of a referendum (astonishingly only the third in British history) – all votes count, thus all are equal; that of the Prime Minister is of no greater potency than the one cast by a young person exercising their franchise for the first time.

Passions were high at the start of the campaign, and got ever more elevated. Generally mutual respect and tolerance of others' feelings held sway, but feuds and rifts did develop, often between colleagues, even friends. The debate itself lurched from the brilliant to the banal, the dogmatic to the pragmatic, the profound to the ludicrous.

There were claims from both sides which were almost invariably countered – prophesies of doom if we voted for Brexit, matched by predictions of Utopia from the 'out' group if the shackles of Brussels were cast aside.

Then came the figures – the financial forecasts – a tsunami of such; rarely has the saying that there are 'lies, damned lies and statistics' been more apt.

For to glean from either side numbers of even remote accuracy was harder than finding a manager who can lead the England football team to glory. From both camps would come claims in terms of the financial benefits or calamities which would come the way of the nation if Brexit came about; nothing wrong with this in theory, but the problem was that virtually every sum quoted had noughts added, or subtracted, depending on which flight of fancy aided the argument put forward by the propagandist.

The debate dominated parliament and the media. It also loomed large in pubs, shops and people's front rooms; fervour abounded – though it never really got out of control (after all, we are British and usually keep our emotions in check, except for football of course).

Then came the vote, the result and the unavoidable recriminations and disputes; nothing here though that time cannot heal. One aspect of the exercise did, however, disappoint – the turnout. It is said that some five million did not register to vote at all, and of those who did, 72 per cent exercised their franchise; thus over a quarter did not. Clearly their right, of course, but none of them should have the nerve to complain about the result. Sadly, many will – vociferously.

58

Pessimism

*T*HERE are few things in this life possessed by others which I envy – but I would be rare in the world if there was nothing. Occasionally, I feel a twinge of it when hearing that somebody has written a bestseller, or have suddenly come into the kind of wealth which would secure the future of our family and ourselves for decades to come – but it is minimal.

What I do crave, however – on occasions at least – is not something material but an attitude of mind; as a lifelong pessimist of Herculean proportions, I long to be an optimist – even for a day. Mind you, it is not altogether my fault that I am very much a 'glass half empty' man (and that's on a good day); for I was born into a long standing farming family, and finding an optimist among those who make their living from the land is about as easy as locating a diamond in a coal mine. Such is understand-able to a degree, for when one's living, no matter how great and assiduous one's own efforts, is so often decided by the vagaries – often sheer bloody mindedness – of weather, it is most difficult to do other than feel that fate is, essentially, a malevolent force perpetually waiting in the wings to wreak mischief. Although I have never actually farmed for a living, this countryman's mindset has ever been with me.

Having said this it is possible that with willpower and a major marshalling of the spirit which made our nation great, I might have been able to throw off this shroud of fatalistic defeatism; unfortunately, an even more potent force took up arms against viewing the future with hope and positivity – at a very young age I became a supporter of Plymouth Argyle; so ended any chance of a buoyant, upbeat attitude to life. One, of course, should not abandon dreams; it could be that one morning I will awaken, see an azure coloured sky with the sun beating down and anticipate a lovely day rather than invoking the downcast approach: 'Too bright, too early', thereby assuming rain. Also, perhaps I'll set off on a journey without the dismal conviction that the car will break down half-way to our destination; the fact that such happens so exceptionally rarely does nothing to eradicate such foolishness.

Then there is leisure and entertainment; I enjoy holidays, visiting the theatre, going out for meals and the like – but usually it is only following the event I feel it has been time well spent, that I am conscious of a sense of contentment. Why cannot I feel such prior to it? Why does my outlook have to be dominated by forebodings – the holiday let will be cold, uncomfortable; the play, concert, show boring – the meal unappetising – or, even worse, the service slow?

Probably, most often of all, I pose to myself – sometimes in frustration, possibly even despair – the question, 'Why can't I wake of a Saturday morning in winter with the outlook 'Great – Home Park today; should be a good game?' The reality is, however, that I will trudge about all morning, zombie like, my brain dominated by a doom laden conviction that no matter whom the Pilgrims are playing – it could be a bunch of cub scouts – they will still be able to snatch calamity from the jaws of triumph. It has ever been thus with me, even when I was a lad – and I see no change evolving in the future. Mind you, whilst having this desire to embrace optimism, there are times when I appreciate what, possibly, are benefits – albeit, mild – in the opposite. For does not viewing the future with hope and positivity inevitably make one a hostage to fortune? It is bad enough returning from Home Park following a defeat for the team even when such was anticipated – but would it not be worse if initially one set off to Plymouth in the expectation of witnessing a home win?

And what about that holiday? There is a saying that it is 'often better to travel hopefully than to arrive'; the optimist will journey in such a sanguine way but, should the ultimate destination prove disenchanting, then a feeling of dismay – even anger – might well dominate.

Not so with the pessimist; for he or she will be prepared mentally for disillusionment and, thus, it will be taken in their stride; 'blessed are they who expecteth nothing for they shall not be disappointed'.

Arguably this is a shrewd way to approach life; certainly I cannot see myself shrugging off the ingrained habits of a lifetime – yet it would be great, before I expire, to experience a moment of optimism, if only to see what it feels like.

59

A Miserable Toad

A couple of years ago, one of our sons, for Father's Day, generously presented me with a bottle of Scotch (long since imbibed) and a splendid door stop in the shape of a frog. This sizeable, heavy beast which, in summer, stoically props open a door when there is a through draught, has a very glum expression and, when given me, was described as 'a miserable toad' for a possibly likewise man.

I believe it was meant somewhat 'tongue in cheek' – he still accompanies me to Home Park, anyway, (my patient son, that is, not the doorstop) though there, I have to admit to being a very 'miserable toad' on far too many occasions. Also, I must confess to being a 'grumpy old man' – which all too often comes to the fore in these articles. Despite this, however, I do feel I have a sense of humour; my problem is that modern comedians, situation comedies, chat shows and so forth, rarely locate it.

Thus do I sit gazing blankly, even bemusedly, at a television screen when those around me are falling about with laughter. With all the perception, insight and sense of irony of a dim-witted hamster, I so often need to have 'jokes' explained to me – then often do not find them funny. Banter also frequently passes me by – the interplay between those participating in shows such as *Have I Got News For You*, *Eight Out of Ten Cats*, *QI* and the like, falling on the stoniest ground as far as I am concerned; for me they often appear crude, unpleasant, supercilious, mocking, even cruel but never really witty or funny – and participants seem to be drawn from a miniscule number of men and women, truly an exclusive club.

Then there are the situation comedies. I find watching *Miranda* more painful than doing the weekly grocery shop; is not the success and popularity of Ms Hart as a comedienne amongst life's great mysteries?

A whole cluster of other regulars – *Gavin and Stacey*, *Little Britain*, *Not Going Out*, *Mrs Brown's Boys*, for example – can, with rapidity, make my fingers access the 'off' button. Mind you, even going back a bit *Absolutely Fabulous*, *Fawlty Towers* and *Some Mothers Do 'Ave 'Em* were, I feel, boring and unfunny – keeping good company here with, to me, surprisingly lauded and much watched American imports such as *Cheers*, *Friends*, *Seinfeld*, and back even further, *MASH*.

Likewise comedians of both genders; Billy Connelly, though a sound actor, is, in my jaundiced opinion, most unentertaining. Lenny Henry, Jo Brand, and assuredly, her namesake Russell, are to me about as amusing as a toothache. So many modern comedians seem bereft of genuine wit and talent, relying all too often on bad language – surely a poor substitute for humour.

Still, 'miserable toad' though I am, I have found situation comedies and performers funny in the past. I could sit for

"A miserable toad for a possibly likewise man."

hours watching re-runs of *Only Fools and Horses*, and still enjoy them; also *Jeeves and Wooster*, with Hugh Laurie and Stephen Fry – great viewing. *Porridge* is another sit-com, which, one feels, has travelled well, whilst some of the sketches from Morecambe and Wise remain masterpieces of entertainment; and going back even further, the machinations of Phil Silvers as *Sergeant Bilko* are memorable.

Some old comedians and performers, also, were priceless; Kenneth William, with his remarkable range of voices and accents; before that, Cyril Fletcher with his 'Odd Odes' – which could be quite brilliant. Max Bygraves too with his catch phrase 'I Want to Tell You a Story'; he could do just that – and often it was funny; he could belt out a decent song, as well. Then there is the legendary Ken Dodd – still performing regularly into his eighties – and a brace of stand up comics, sadly no longer here to enliven us; the Irishman, Frank Carson, with his quick-fire jokes 'It's the way I tell 'em' – could be a delight, whilst the great Les Dawson, always was. To me he was the funniest man ever I saw and I never tire of seeing his old shows, hearing the jokes which, heard so often, I almost know by heart; despite their familiarity, however, they remain hilarious – truly a comic genius, a man who could raise a smile, indeed, a guffaw, in most of use even when we are faced with the 'slings and arrows of outrageous fortune'. It is unlikely we will see his like again.

However, I have still not given up hope of turning on the television one day in the near future and seeing a young comic of either gender who can lift me to a facial expression less morose than that upon our forlorn doorstop.

60

Blow Your Own Trumpet

IN his sermon on the mount, Jesus stated that 'the meek shall inherit the earth'. Clearly that eminent lyricist William S. Gilbert – whose claim to lasting fame is in his successful partnership with Arthur Sullivan in the masterly series of 19th century comic operas – was of diametrically opposed views.

For he saw no future in diffidence or modesty, exemplified by his well known quote – 'If you wish in this universe to advance, your merits you're bound to enhance; you must stir it and stump it and blow your own trumpet or, trust me, you haven't a chance.'

In what is termed 'an ideal world', the teachings of Christ would be the beacon which lights our way; those of gentleness, courtesy, tolerance, who are law abiding, bound by honour and rigid moral code should have immense influence in this life – should shape it and the way we live; success should be theirs also, if they match such attributes with talent, ability and endeavour.

However, observation of the world about us, and that of the past, suggests the 'meek' rarely gain their just rewards

– they certainly do not appear to 'inherit the earth'. It could be that Mr Gilbert, a most gifted man, would have been carried to the heights by his brilliance without being a 'blower' (to use the Devonshire word for the braggart), but he might have been overlooked – so many people of flair, originality and creativity, even those gifted with genius, can, if shrouded by self-effacing modesty, be outflanked by those of less talent but vastly superior abilities in self promotion.

Often such prominence can come simply by someone thrusting themselves into public view – in this day and age probably through the medium of reality television, *Big Brother* for example; for here, no real talent is involved, rather a willingness to abandon virtually all ideas of privacy in pursuit of fame (though so often 'notoriety' would be more apt).

Also there are shows such as *The X-Factor* watched by millions; whilst clearly there are some contestants with real talent, a number are but shameless exhibitionists. Many are eliminated early on but others whose behaviour, often grotesque, somehow pleases a number of viewers, survive vastly longer than they should; they become so called 'celebrities' and make a lot of money from it. A lady who enjoyed relatively little limelight in a field where she was most able (politics), Ann Widdecombe, went on, after she had retired from the House of Commons, to fame and possibly fortune following her headline grabbing appearances in *Strictly Come Dancing* – where she was dire. Democracy reigning, she remained in the competition because viewers kept voting her back; indeed she, who had the dancing ability and the fleetness of foot

of a whelk, remained – bringing despair to the judg
when so many of infinitely greater ability had been :
home; assuredly she 'stirred it and stumped it' and
worked superbly.

Then there was ski-jumper Eddie 'The Eagle' Edwards
who achieved quite phenomenal publicity – fame also –
some years ago. Clearly a courageous man (it is no sport
for the faint-hearted), he, unfortunately, seemed not to be
gifted with great ability on the piste. Yet by virtue of
personality, undoubted charisma, persistence and adept
self-promotion, he succeeded in dominating headlines,
often receiving far more coverage than did the champions
of his chosen sport; he remains a well known name even
today.

A number of others spring to mind in so many
prominent walks of life – from show business to politics –
with little ability or accomplishment – who have seized
upon William Gilbert's exhortation, and adroitly enhanced
what little, if any, merits they possess.

Mind you, despite all these motley folk who fervently
avoid 'hiding their light under a bushel', the British
remain essentially a modest race – understatement,
generally, still holds sway. Across the Atlantic, however,
there dwells a race with a somewhat different approach.
Americans are brasher; self effacement is not necessarily
seen as a virtue. If someone is good at something then why
not tell the world? Muhammad Ali was a master of this in
his early years – and assuredly it gave him the chance to
'advance'; equally certain, he had the ability to take it.
Observation, though, would suggest there is no shortage of
Yanks who possess confidence in themselves perhaps not

211

their abilities or accomplishments.
example of this (though time will tell)
al arena; his first name is Donald, his
s vividly the personal instrument which Mr
should be blown; he is astonishingly good at
and it might take him to the White House.

(Written on 20th October 2016 – weeks before
Donald Trump was elected President of the USA.)